NEW DIRECTIONS IN THE I CHING

THE YELLOW RIVER LEGACY

New Directions in the I Ching

The Yellow River Legacy

by
Larry Schoenholtz

Foreword by Leslie Shepard
Illustrations by Gayle Murray

UNIVERSITY BOOKS

Secaucus, New Jersey

Contents

Foreword by Leslie Shepard 7

Preface 13

PART ONE – BASIC CONCEPTS AND HISTORY OF THE *I CHING*
   (1) The *Tao* As She Is Spoke 23
   (2) Song of the Sacred Yarrow Plant 45
   (3) The Principle of Synchronicity 61

PART TWO–TECHNICAL RELATIONS AMONG HEXA-GRAMS
   (4) The Nuclear Concept of Change 75
   (5) Primary and Secondary Relationships 89
   (6) Hexagram Families 99

PART THREE – FREE RELATIONS AMONG HEXAGRAMS
   (7) Freedom and the Moving Line 113
   (8) Creativity and Change 125
   Postscript 135

SUPPLEMENTARY MATERIAL

Appendix A – Divination Methods 141
Appendix B – Mathematical Calculations 145
Appendix C – Schematic Design for the DNR-16 149
Bibliography 151
Index 153

Foreword

Barely a decade ago, a great wave of disillusionment with the affluent society swept over American campuses, and thousands of young people suddenly reacted in startling ways that represented a complete break with former academic tradition. Some became violent protesters against war, political and social revolutionaries; others drugged themselves to idiocy in a search for inner freedom that became a tragic slavery to a habit. Still others took up Eastern religions and occultism in a romantic reaction against materialistic society.

Today, the violent campus confrontations have died down, and the sensible addicts have kicked the drug habit, much as their parents quit smoking. But the quest for the soul and its symbols in occultism and Eastern mysticism still continues and may be here to stay.

Among partly trendy, partly sincere avocations like astrology and the Tarot cards, one of the most enduring preoccupations has been with the *I Ching,* the ancient Chinese *Book of Changes.*

While the new mass-media pop religions rapidly outdo each other in extravagant claims, Maharishis, Gurujis, and Krishna Consciousness rising and falling in the charts, the dedication to the less sensational mysteries of the *I Ching* grows steadily. Among many thousands of kids who merely got on a bandwagon, there has also been a solid core of intelligent allegiance, and many individuals have taken the *I Ching* as seriously as a Master's course and found new insights through it.

Larry Schoenholtz is one of those intelligent young men. He grew up with astrology and the *I Ching* and brought a keen, alert mind to bear on these ancient systems. I knew him when he was a college kid, trying to assimilate Eastern transcendentalism and Western sexual pressures (a formidable equation at any age). He stayed outside the trendy nonconformism of his own generation, something that took courage and an independent judgment. His natural talent for music and astrology kept alive a romantic interest in the *I Ching,* but his keen, restless intellect led him into the new directions described in this book.

One of the things he taught me about the *I Ching* (for I was a novice in its ways) is that you must respect its methods and ritual. He avoided the noisy, indiscriminate, party-games atmosphere in which ancient oracles are usually investigated; instead, he set aside a quiet time and place for inquiry. It was always a pleasure to see the careful, intent way in which he handled the yarrow stalks, still the oldest and best technique. The ritual was a poised gathering together of question and action, consultation and study, in an almost musical pattern. This is as it should be, for the hexagrams are not vulgar fortune-telling, but something to be meditated upon in the spirit of the *Tao,* where intellect and intuition balance each other and life has mystical significance.

It is part of the paradox and eternal flux of the *I Ching* that its most mystical moments have an intricate mathematical basis, and consideration of these structural beauties has led Larry Schoenholtz into deeper areas of study of the *I Ching.* As a result of thousands of careful explorations into the hexagrams and their meanings, he has become aware of fascinating patterns not previously described, new approaches to an understanding of the *I Ching.* I believe that such a deeper knowledge of the structure of the *I Ching* will enhance the intuitive side of consultation.

As every beginner knows, there is a standard method of consulting this oracle, as well as various shortcuts, or "lazy" methods. How far you go beyond that depends only on your ambition and intelligence. Many people are content simply to regard the *I Ching* as a divination game like the tarot pack, but believe me, there is much more to it than that.

What the author of this book has done is to go beyond the simple divination method into considerations of geometry, mathematics, and higher meanings in the *I Ching.* The book will open up new avenues for the serious student who wishes to go beyond the elementary stage of casual consultation.

I am pleased that the *I Ching* still grows in popularity, particularly among young people, and I would like to see more adults taking an interest in its philosophy. Part of its appeal lies in the apparently endless depths of basic structure and metaphysical insight that it reveals.

Perhaps this may not attract those who only want a quick, superficial system of fortune-telling, but it is a system that any intelligent person may study without feeling intellectually embarrassed. The more closely one investigates the *I Ching,* the more richness one finds. After more than two thousand years of life in the East, it now begins a new era in the West.

There are two major English translations, either or both of which should be studied and used side by side with the present work. There is the well-known version of C. F. Baynes, with a foreword by Professor C. G. Jung, that describes the concept of synchronicity, the acausal linkage of events that seems to underlie such occult arts as astrology and the *I Ching*. There is also the excellent translation by James Legge, first published 1882.

Both versions have been reprinted from time to time and are currently available. Of the two, the Legge is perhaps the most accurate, even if the author seems to be uncomfortable about divination. This edition is available from University Books, Inc., Secaucus, New Jersey. The Wilhelm-Baynes edition is of value primarily for its Jung orientation.

Most people who have experimented with the *I Ching* agree that careful consultation yields devastatingly accurate indications and insights. The skeptical say this is because the text is sufficiently ambiguous to mean anything (this is not true, as you may find for yourself), but they respect the fantastic mathematical basis and the fascinating scheme of sequences.

I believe that the *I Ching* is more revealing in its insights than the tarot, but it must be consulted in a proper frame of mind, as a ritual. The ritual is as much a matter of respect and mental concentration as a religious service and can also yield joy and understanding. In using the *I Ching* one is inquiring into the nature of things and the destiny of one's soul rather than fortune-telling.

I believe that this new book will take beginners a big step forward in their appreciation of the beauty and wisdom of the *I Ching.* It is a heartening sign to me that people are finding new dimensions in a great system now more than two thousand years old.

It is perhaps ironic that at the peak of modern China's cultural revolution, folklore and piety have been transformed into the secular religion of Maoism, and the *I Ching* and Confucius now take second place to Western technology. At the same moment in time, the Western countries have become tired of mere technology, and thousands of intelligent people now turn to an ancient Chinese metaphysical and divination system no longer given first place in the land of its birth.

It may well be that New China will make a great success of its adaptation of Western technology, and perhaps the West will bring a deeper metaphysical impulse to its technology by study of the marvelous *I Ching* from Ancient China.

I hope that both will make new discoveries.

Leslie Shepard

Preface

Somewhere between thirty and fifty centuries ago, in the vicinity of the Yellow River, a mysterious folk hero by the name of Fu Hsi left an equally mysterious document known as the Yellow River Map.

According to one version of the legend, a magic tortoise crawled onto the bank where Fu Hsi sat and presented him with what eventually became known as the eight trigrams. Each of the trigrams was cryptically inscribed on the tortoise's shell. Another version of the legend claims that Fu Hsi was himself a magical being and that he devised the eight trigrams in a single sitting's contemplation of heaven and earth.

Whatever the true source of the *I Ching* may be, we do know that it was already considered to be an ancient work by the time Confucius studied it a couple of hundred years before Christ. And although we may be unclear about the remotest history of this great classic, it is quite safe to say that the depth of the *I Ching* has never been exhausted and perhaps never will be. However, the historical attempt to do so has been very fruitful. From Confucius and his school to Richard and Hellmut Wilhelm, various lights have been thrown upon the body of the text, lights that are masterpieces in themselves. Undoubtedly, many more are yet to come — the *I Ching* invites them. Being both a work of extreme mathematical conciseness and a pool of poetry and intuitive energy, the *Book of Changes* cannot help but seduce the curious searcher within us.

Although the *Book of Changes* was designed (or certainly evolved) to be a system for oracle consultation, a person doesn't have to accept this aspect in order to derive benefit from it. For to the extent that the *I Ching* is a book of wisdom as well as a book of oracles, it holds organic possibilities for all human beings. Experience has shown me, however, that the *Book of Changes* is probably better appreciated as an oracle. I realize that this aspect of it is quite a bitter pill for Rational Humanity to swallow. But I am in many ways myself a member of this breed; yet with only a token dose of faith, I was able to swallow the pill, and experience digested it for me. Admittedly, I was perhaps very fortunate in the results I obtained in the first dozen or so encounters with the system. Others may or may not be so fortunate – the *I Ching can* be confusing at times. I only suggest that any person who can appreciate it as a book of wisdom also give it a try as a book of oracles.

Years of intimate work with the text and system of the *I Ching* have led me through some unusual and hopeful new portals. And I have been very careful. Since the wise men have always put slippers on their words in discussing the *Book of Changes*, I have been inclined to wear no covering at all. The somewhat daring intention of attempting to bring fresh spirits out of a thirty-century-old bottle is a delicate enough issue, without committing the sin of insensitivity. What I have to offer through the discoveries in this work I present very much in the spirit of inquiry. The *I Ching* is not something I wish to petrify in abstraction. I feel much more like simply an attentive gardener in the vast vale of the Changes – one who desires little more than an opportunity to give you a good view of one particular corner of it that may have been neglected.

The intermediate student of the *I Ching* can benefit most from my book. The novice would do well to obtain a good translation of the original text first (I highly recommend Richard Wilhelm's translation), rather than to plunge immediately into the comparatively obscure notions presented here. However, the novice has not been neglected in these pages. The first three chapters and the postscript can be read as matters of general interest surrounding the philosophy and history of the *I Ching.* For the student of the Changes who is not a novice but who has an abhorrence for mathematical details, I have removed as many of the calculations as possible from the material pertinent to chapters four and five and placed them in the appendixes. The particularly creative and intuitive student will undoubtedly derive the greatest benefit from the last three chapters, the very last of which is especially designed for him or her.

It is impossible, of course, to acknowledge everyone who contributes to a work of this sort. Such a list would have to include scores of individuals who assisted in the production of this work in a small (but necessary) way, as well as those who "merely" encouraged my spiritual development as man and artist. These people especially have only a passing acquaintance with the *I Ching* and are the people to whom I am most indebted. I'm glad you all know who you are.

There are always the people deserving of specific mention, however. I am first of all thankful to two old friends who were there years ago when the concepts of this work were being formed and who helped to create or direct the course of these ideas: Dennis Kocienda and Dale Guciardi. I am grateful to Mike Kuczajda, who gave my sixteen system its first good, long-range test on the subjective level. He had faith in it almost before I did!

I would particularly like to thank David Vest for his computer schematic based on the new system, and Gayle Murray for her eight magnificent ink drawings. I've promised to write Gayle an even better book the next time around. Finally, I would like to express my deepest gratitude to Leslie Shepard, without whose persistent insight, advice, and encouragement this work would never have been produced.

Larry Schoenholtz

Detroit, Michigan
August 1, 1974

when immersed in the flow of the tao,
the pattern is everything.

PART ONE

* *

BASIC CONCEPTS AND HISTORY OF THE I CHING

CHAPTER ONE

The *Tao* As She Is Spoke

To understand the somewhat intimate world of the *I Ching,* it is first of all necessary to have at least a partial grasp of the philosophy of life that grew up with the great classic. By the term *philosophy* I am not referring to what we normally mean by the term. The philosophy of ancient China was not at all an intellectual body of platitudes and conceptual frameworks. It was a completely organic conglomeration of folk wisdom and oral tradition. Stretching far back into the animism and magic of primitive China, it grew into the highly sophisticated theosophical systems of such figures as Confucius and Lao-tse. We now tend to group this particular set of ideas and perceptions under the general notion "philosophy of the *Tao*." Not to be confused with Taoism itself, the philosophy of the *Tao* runs like a golden thread through most of the world's religions and philosophies. Through understanding this thread, the world of the *I Ching* becomes accessible.

But what is this little three-letter word *"Tao"*? This is good question, since it has no precise translation into any of our Western languages. Some have called it "universal flow" or "flow of nature." D. T. Suzuki says that the Tao is "that for which there is nothing beyond." I have, on occasion, also seen it translated as "God" or "Mother Nature," though I'm fairly convinced that such liberties of translation can only add to the confusion of the matter. It is also no great stretch of the imagination to see that Henri Bergson's *"élan vital"* or Gopi Krishna's "evolutionary energy" might be suitable. One might as well suggest Einstein's "unified field," too. I find "flow of nature" satisfying enough.

One thing that is somewhat true of all these partial abstractions is that the notion of a bridge is involved — looking at the *Tao* as simply a bridge between the past and the future, for instance, or between being and nonbeing. Lao-tse often referred to the *Tao* as the synthesis of opposites. Whatever kind of bridge the *Tao* represents, one point is fundamentally clear — any talk of bridges is a talk concerning humankind. Humankind is *the* bridge-builder of the earth. Bridge talk has always been humanity's special shoptalk.

Since the dawn of consciousness, our species has seemingly always been caught a little short on action. We have spent at least as much time arguing about how to act as we have spent acting. Before the dawn of reflection (if there ever was such a time), things pretty much took care of themselves. There was absolutely no need to seek out a particular means of survival through a *philosophy* of actions. This altogether peculiar need to "suspend" ourselves through value-action philosophies is of incredibly recent vintage. Suspension by itself had always done just fine. The web, the nest, drives and instincts — even conditioned learning patterns — take care of themselves, no questions asked. The unconscious bursts, spasms, quirks, quacks, and wiggles of prereflective life were the automatically guaranteed bridges of existence. There was no fuss and muss about "choices" and "systems" — just a lot of tooth and nail, with particular blends of strength, chance, and endurance determining the outcome. But with the (alleged) dawn of reflection, the automatic became somehow replaced by a restless and relentless search for psychic bridges.

Not being an anthropologist, I hope the reader will forgive me for glossing over the precise details of man's early transitions as they are now believed to have happened. What concerns me is simply the brute fact that reflection has come to be so entwined with culture that we can hardly imagine living our lives without substantial reimbursements of reflective thought. The results are not altogether favorable.

Of course, the bridges that I am talking about are wholly psychic bridges. When the human mind comes to a difficult impasse — difficult because it is either unknown or unsuspected — the first impulse is nearly always to span it. If reflection is to deal with it, reflection must construct a suitable bridge. The question of what constitutes a "suitable" bridge not only makes for the rise and fall of civilizations, but propels the imaginations of individuals toward their creative enterprises.

The oldest bridges of the mind are undoubtedly those constructed almost wholly of dogma and ritual. These are the bamboo footbridges of the human condition. What better thing to do when faced with the chaos of existence than to latch on to the artificial suspensions offered by dogma and ritual? Unfortunately, such bridges are satisfactory only in homogeneous cultures. When an entire society has exactly the same kind of environmental concerns — when survival means precisely the same thing to each member of the culture — dogma and ritual can be the very cement of life. Whether this be an African tribe, a Gothic village, or a small community hidden far back in the Ozarks, the ends of unity

26

and order are served very effectively by the local dogmas and rituals. (Rebels and outsiders, of course, are not part of this homogeneous framework.)

In heterogeneous cultures, dogma and ritual tend to work far less effectively. In an electronic-media culture such as ours, for instance, pure population pressure makes a mockery of such unifying structures. This is not to say, of course, that we do not have our own dogmas and rituals — only that we are constantly barraged by alternatives. Despite any good show of ritualization (fad and law being the first two that come to my mind), the fact remains that our society is, by and large, culturally schizophrenic. We are all insiders and outsiders, conformists and rebels at the same time.

We all possess different balances of these alternatives, sometimes only in subtle degrees, and this fact points to one clear truth — the breakdown of dogma and ritual as effective bridges in the human condition is accompanied by increased individualization. For some mysterious reason, however (perhaps only because of a nostalgic yearning to be one again), the individualization of man is opposed on nearly all fronts of the mind. The desire to perpetuate a human *image* seems almost inexhaustible.

And so we come to science. *Objectivity* is an effective enough synonym for our purposes. It is one of the great ironies of history that the Renaissance, that great torchbearer for individualization, did a lot as well to circumvent the true emergence of individuality. What it so annoyingly and unsuspectingly fostered was a movement to make the ultimate dogma from the ingredients of reason and science. What started as a simple attempt to remove humanity from the center of the universe ended in an obsession to drive us from the universe altogether. It is no great secret, for instance, that people who have had great subjective visions have had to promote those visions *against* the grain of the so-called scientific spirit.

Intuitions and inspirations of every sort have been required to fit the mold of rational syllogisms in order to stand on a respectable footing. With one wide swoop, most of the teachings of great medieval alchemists have been laid to rest. After nearly forty years of good research to the contrary, Webster's dictionary still defines astrology as a pseudo-science. Granted, the paranoia of the early Renaissance thinkers was well founded. Anyone who had a significant idea in the early days of free thought was bound to have the hot breath of the Inquisition breathing down her or his neck. But why make a science of paranoia? Now we have the equally cold breath of the scientific community to contend with.

The trouble with the scientific method, as with religious dogma before it, is that it does not permit one to say *enough*. The ghost of "objective proof" is always present to attempt to sterilize our gropings by forcing its demands upon them. Acting as a sort of psychic meat grinder, it can leave us little room for faith in things that are essentially invisible or unprovable. Sometimes we are fools with blind faith and petty daydreams, and sometimes we are fools with great visions. The particular shortcoming of objectivity is that it is completely impotent when called upon to make this fundamental distinction.

Emerson once said, "All our progress is an unfolding like the vegetable bud. You have first an instinct, then an opinion, then a knowledge, as the plant has root, bud, and fruit. Trust the instinct to the end though you can render no reason." If all our visions could be rendered reasons, humankind would be beating its drum to our tune. But it is hardly so easy a process.

We spend great amounts of energy learning to discriminate among our instincts before finding the ones worth seeing through to a higher end. And we must do this though everyone about us descend quickly upon us with their microscopes and data sheets. One may eventually come to grips with an important subjective truth. What is not objectively reconciled becomes someone else's nightmare. For there is an implicit request in the objectivist attitude that is dead false. Just as no one can *answer* for all humankind, neither can anyone *ask* for all humankind — and that is the implicit request of objectivity.

There are characteristics common to our whole race — matters like eating, sleeping, and longevity — that objectivity may help to classify and raise to the level of a universal law. But there are also characteristics, completely peculiar to each member of our species, that are laws unto themselves. It is for the sake of this latter, highly untapped reservoir that we should, at least occasionally, understand when objectivity belongs to the realm of sincere and wholesome approaches or to the realm of dogma and ritual. It simply makes no sense, for instance, to say that a human body is objectively 99.9999999 percent empty (because the atoms that comprise it are) when that body casts a shadow that is 100 percent full.

Let objectivity make a more endurable carpet or write a more precise history. In the community of human beings — more particularly in the community inside a human being — let this half-god, half-hobgoblin take its place with its fellow ghosts and seekers.

The reader may wonder what all this has to do with the philosophy of the *Tao,* much less with the *I Ching.* The answer is that the philosophy of the *Tao* is a bridge — a superbridge, if you will — that attempts to reconcile all previous and subbridges.

The *Tao* is a grand enterprise seeking to fuse the best of both the subjective and objective worlds of the collective human soul. It is religious in tone without being at all antiscientific; it is science with feeling.

The core idea of the philosophy of the *Tao* is the mode and discipline by which an individual attains a lasting commitment to peace of mind. Peace of mind is not considered to be of much worth these days. However, with the lasting peace of mind promised by attuning oneself with the discipline of this philosophy, one may step through the world without error. The person who, traditionally, has been recognized as a person of the *Tao* is one who has purged the common anxieties of consciousness without sacrificing a single aspect that might be considered virtuous. He or she is fun loving, disciplined, inquisitive, compassionate, and a master at bringing forth the best in people. I find these qualities not only in Taoism and its related systems (like Zen Buddhism), but also in most of the world's religions, theosophical movements, and philosophies concerned with defining the "good" or "just" person.

In a letter written to me by Leslie Shepard, I noted a passage that suggested the type of peace of which the *Tao* speaks: "If any of us do a little that is done well, with integrity, if we use whatever influence we have in our immediate surroundings for quiet sanity and rationality, if we simply shut off from the noise level of irrational infantile potty-smashing and dirtying all over the carpet, our lives will not be in vain." That passage embodies much that is spoken in the spirit of the *Tao*.

Let us examine the notion of peace a bit further. *Peace* is not a word like *cyclotron*. It is a word like *love.* It is virtually undefinable in terms that can be exactly conveyed to another person. When one recognizes that the word *peace* has, in our era, become so loosely defined that phrases like *kill for peace* or *peace with honor in Vietnam* are considered legitimate usages, one must realize that we have stretched the meaning of the word to its ultimate limits.

The peace of the *Tao* is the great reward humanity seeks for its labors. It is far more than the peace of safety or "predictability" that have been more commonly accepted as the real definitions of peace. Let me add the notion of "national security" to those meanings as well. The peace of the *Tao* is far more deep and lasting. If we are to place any trust whatever in the teachings of great Eastern sages, there is no richer reward for life's struggles than this peace. So it is ironic that this peace itself cannot be received.

Why is this so? For one thing, peace itself has come to be distrusted. Many look at *peace* as another word for *apathy.* But Lao-tse never meant that a person of peace be a nonparticipating, mountain-bound recluse — though it is commonly asserted that he did. He did realize that this could be one sincere and legitimate alternative. By and large, however, I feel he realized that the great majority of people would always be eager to participate in the social intercourse of life. And to them, too, he offered the

Tao of peace. If one acts from the heart of peace, thought the great sage, one can never be entrapped in the hysteria of life. One can gracefully accept life *so that* one can pour her or his own kind of nectars back into the flow. A person can then exist as a pure bridge between the vast worlds of impression and expression, letting his or her peace of mind act as a filter between the two.

Coupled with this confused joining of peace and apathy is an underlying feeling that is perhaps far more to the point–peace is temperamentally dull to modern eyes. Modern humanity has come to be little more than the atoms which make up so large a part of its being. We are quick and hysterical, like atoms in a cloud chamber, occasionally making bonds and collisions here and there, always at breakneck pace. There is a collective nervousness about us that I think would look as funny to a man of ancient rural China as the high-speed action of the early motion pictures looks to us. To a person of the *Tao* especially, contemporary life might appear like people jumping on hot coals trying to shake ants out of each other's pants. Next to all these hot particulars of the "rat race," the quiet sense of serene finality offered by the *Tao* is altogether too "boring."

A third reason — perhaps the most important — that modern humanity tends to shirk the peace of the *Tao* is that such peace seems so much like death. This is a somewhat reasonable fear. Our cosmological training has been geared in such a manner that this is indeed the case. To be a fully working unit in the "flow of nature," assert the *Tao*-minded, the ego must eventually dissolve. This is not really the same as death as we have so morbidly defined it.

When I mentioned earlier that science has been obsessed with removing humanity from the universe, I was not quite precise in my choice of words. It would be far more fair and correct to say that science has been concerned with narrowing the concept of life as much as possible. It could amount to the same thing in the end, if the concept is so narrowed that human beings no longer qualify. B. F. Skinner may have done this already, depending on your choice of definitions and your feelings in the matter. I think science supposes that it has accomplished a great feat in declaring man "alive and conscious," an insect "alive but unconscious," and a river or mountain "inanimate, lifeless matter." This is too funny to be considered even preposterous.

Who was the first person to declare a river dead? As self-respecting animists a quarter of a million years ago, we quite possibly didn't think of *anything* as dead. The average scientist today doesn't recognize anything "preamoebic" as having "life." This probably eliminates all but .00000000000000000000001 percent of existence in the universe. Hydrogen and helium make up the greater bulk of all that deadness.

Amazing! It is so rare a thing to possess life that I can almost feel myself instinctively taking larger gulps of air to make sure I go on having it. This is silly, of course — superstition in full bloom. But scientists have been no less arbitrary in defining this mysterious golden spook called life than the Taoists have been in claiming, "All is life." The Taoists, however, are only too aware of their arbitrariness.

The Taoist view is not "right" — it is simply more practical, more encompassing, and far less anxiety inducing than the Western scientific view. It's no great wonder that twentieth-century technology grew side by side with the emergence of the absurdist-existentialist, anguish-saturated, nausea-associated schools of nihilism. With the proportion of human life in the universe being less than one part per decillion parts of emptiness and inanimacy, it's no wonder at all. Modern humanity has simply made a fetish of human form.

Call it humanism, if you will — it is still unhealthy from a metaphysical viewpoint. To the Taoist, a good corpse is as good as a good worm — the pattern is everything. It is a distinct shame that we couldn't sit Jean-Paul Sartre and Lao-tse together in the same room. Would that be a tutelage! Sartre would be crying, "Everything is nothing!" and Lao-tse would be replying, "Yes, but nothing is everything!"

While we are on the subject of arbitrating the line

between life and death, let me illustrate the matter with a hypothetical fantasy. Modern science claims that life appeared on this planet about a billion or so years ago. Well, let us suppose that it is more or less a universal law that any consciousness in the universe can recognize the special ingredient called life only if the form it perceives is within a billion or so years of its own development.

That is, suppose there are no Taoists in the Alpha Centauri system. Suppose there are only creatures like modern scientists throughout the universe. Now imagine that these creatures are more than a billion years ahead of us in evolution (and there are plenty of stars that much older than our sun). In visiting our planet, what do you suppose they would find? The answer is simple — nothing. A bunch of rocks. They could walk down Wall Street during the rush hour and, with their most sensitive instruments, not find even the slightest hints of life. Maybe they might encounter an Einstein or a Beethoven and recognize the first amoebic twinklings of life. Maybe not. They might very well deduce that life has not yet appeared on the third planet of our star system, and move on to Venus or Mars. I might be inclined to agree with them at times, I should add. The joke "Is there really life after birth?" is perhaps not all that funny.

But of course it is! That's the whole Taoist point, and they would be the first to laugh. As a matter of fact, Taoism has traditionally been voted the religion most likely to enjoy a good joke. One always runs across laughing figures in the early Taoist ink scrolls, for instance. The reason that this is so — that any serious discussion among the Tao minded could dissolve into cosmic laughter — is that the Taoists are much freer from the anxieties of consciousness than most of the rest of us. They are freer because they have trained themselves not to be driven to, by, from, for, or with anything not of their choosing. They have, in a very real sense, already died — or they have always been alive. It all depends upon how broadly and with what attitude one looks upon it.

Returning to our original line of discussion, we have only to make a direct statement now: As long as Western humanity clings to the ship of our highly specialized, highly localized, highly fragile ego, we will always be at least a little bit paranoid. Not being very intimately connected with much beyond our own skin, we will continue to float like a bug in the vast ocean of emptiness and alien substance about us. We have, indeed, made almost a nightmare of the smallness and isolation our cosmology has afforded us. And, hanging only a hair away from being crushed by this vastness at any moment, why should we affiliate ourselves with a philosophy that claims to eradicate that hair of difference?

The answer is because it works both ways. True,

the universe can crush in and send this poverty-stricken consciousness hurtling down the corridors of death and alienation. But, however poor, this same consciousness can also expand into the universe. Five thousand years of private research has confirmed this claim. Consciousness has as much power to crush nothingness in the universe as nothingness has to crush consciousness. It is not easy, and it does require shedding certain arbitrary notions about life, death, and mind, but it is most certainly possible.

Between the hither and the thither, so to speak, falls the *I Ching.* For the person who is totally in tune with nature, the *I Ching* is superfluous — at best, an aesthetic curiosity. It is supposed that people completely in accord with the *Tao* have no need for oracle consultation because either they already know the outcome of their actions through a highly trained intuitive sense or they simply couldn't care less, feeling that they can do absolutely no better than they are already doing.

On the other hand, with those who have not yet realized how much more valuable are deep intuitions and inspirations than simple perceptions and abstract logic, we can only say that they are not yet ripe for such a tool. For that is what the *I Ching* is more than anything else — a tool. Through its cryptic images and antique advice, it assists open-minded apprentices and helps them in coming to terms with their unconscious workings.

It is well-known that the unconscious in man (some call it the subconscious) stores far more information received through the senses than is readily available to consciousness. Psychoanalysis is one of the methods by which the West attempts to bring this secret and powerful reservoir forth into the light of day. The *I Ching* happens to be the East's way of attempting the same thing. Although the East and the West both realize that the unconscious mind is where things *really* happen in influencing a person's life, the East's idea is a bit more involved.

The East supposes that the unconscious mind not only generates the ideas and motivations that continually conjure up the present state of consciousness, but also has a grasp on the immediate future. Only in recent times has the West come around to this notion. Through Carl Jung's investigations into the "collective unconscious" and through parapsychological research that supports the idea, it is now considered plausible to Western thinkers that the unconscious minds of people are mutually connected in some way — especially those of people who are in intimate social contact with one another.

Therefore, when one brings a question before the *I Ching,* there is more to it than meets the eye. One is not merely presenting a conscious inquiry before the oracle. One is also involving one's unconscious mind and the conscious and unconscious minds of everyone one deals with in day-to-day existence.

It must be perfectly understood that the *I Ching* in

no way predicts the future in some mysteriously magical manner. Mysterious, yes, but in no way magical. When the numerical distribution of the yarrow stalks is counted through, the full content of one's present state and present *potential* is taken into account. The *I Ching* no more reads the future than an aptitude test forecasts an occupation. The reader ought to digest this idea very carefully before we discuss the *hows* of this mystery in chapter three.

One of the most interesting facets of the *I Ching* is that it can be approached as easily from the existential standpoint as from the mystical. By this I mean that it can swing easily and freely across that gulf of the human consciousness which normally separates truths of the greatest universal importance from life's pettiest trivialities. It arises from the unity of phenomena but addresses itself to the duality. This peculiar ease of movement and grace gives the *I Ching* its particular flavor. It recognizes duality as an illusion in the last analysis but takes great pains all the same to cater to the human mind's taste for it.

As I have already said, the *I Ching* was molded into its present shape for no more reason than simply to assist the great number of people temporarily lost in the world of the "ten thousand things." It stands, precisely and immutably, between the grace of action that all of us once possessed as true mammals and this same grace of action as it may be repossessed from the heart of the *Tao*. It stands there with as keen a dignity today as it has had since remotest antiquity.

If my enthusiasm seems a bit keen at times, it is because I have looked into the soul of this enduring dignity and found an altogether worthy teacher. As an altogether worthy student, I bring it before you.

the i ching is a celebration of life

CHAPTER TWO

Song of the Sacred Yarrow Plant

The method by which the *I Ching* is used in oracle consultation is derived from a ritual that is probably almost as old as the text itself. It is known as the yarrow-stalk divination method. A student wishing to bring inquiries before the *I Ching* ought to learn this method well. Of course, in older days, one would simply take one's question before an *I Ching* master rather than perform the ritual oneself. Unfortunately, *I Ching* masters are at a premium these days. In fact, masters in all the occult and semioccult branches of knowledge are now at a premium.

The contemporary climate either no longer permits many such creatures to walk among us or is so infatuated with the fast, prefabricated "answer" that few people have the patience to deal with an individual of the highest possible dedication.

Perhaps we are simply so wary of false messiahs —and there have certainly been plenty—that we find it too risky to trust even the concept of a master any more. I honestly don't know.

Whatever the reason, sincere seekers among these branches of knowledge must virtually grope through chaos until they can come to terms with their own resources. This is particularly true with the *I Ching,* since it comes from the other side of the world and the other side of history. (It is also possibly illegal now under China's present political regime.)

It is our good fortune that the *I Ching's* symbols are somewhat fixed by tradition. Astrology, by comparison, is in absolute chaos. For instance, there are at least a dozen theories regarding the proper way to draw up a birth chart. Such controversy regarding so fundamental a matter can be very frustrating. Students are left to pick and choose and experiment for themselves.

With the *I Ching,* controversy exists almost exclusively in the interpretive side of consultation—a far healthier state of things, I feel. Also, the Richard Wilhelm translation of the *Book of Changes* has the added bonus of having been created through Wilhelm's intimate association with the great *I Ching* master Lao Nai-hsüan.

To return to the yarrow-stalk divination method — it derives its name from the plant from which the stalks are picked. The yarrow plant grows on almost every continent and flourishes in a wide number of varieties. Traditionally, the stalks were picked only from yarrow plants growing on sacred ground (such as on the burial grounds of Confucius and other notable teachers). However, for the essential performance of the ritual, it makes little difference where the stalks grew.

In fact, it is really not even necessary that the fifty sticks used be yarrow. Yarrow stalks happen to be good because they are smooth, round, hard, and straight, but it is not even truly necessary to use sticks. I have used blocks, pennies, paper clips, marbles, pebbles, pencils, toothpicks, scraps of paper, and blueberries (which have the extra advantage of being delightfully consumable while reflecting upon the result).

As long as the fifty items are convenient to manipulate, one is still basically working with the yarrow-stalk divination method. The mathematical ratios that the ancients built into this system (and I will have a good deal more to say about them) are fixed regardless of the medium in which they are used. For the interested student, I have included specific directions for the ritual in Appendix A. It should be remembered, however, that this text is no substitute for a translation of the *Book of Changes.* It is merely an aid. For a reading of the divined hexagram, the student ought to obtain one of the many good translations available (again, Richard Wilhelm's is probably the best).

It is, of course, well recognized that Confucius worked with the *I Ching* rather extensively during the latter part of his life. A famous anecdote (possibly apocryphal, however) claims that Confucius wished that he might have another fifty years added to his life for the sole purpose of devoting more study to the *I Ching.* If this is true, it is a rather impressive statement coming from a great sage who was about ninety at the time.

True or not, Confucius did spend an increasing amount of time with the classic throughout the last decades of his life. His personal contribution to the literature surrounding the Changes appears to be quite extensive, and either he or his school of followers authored more than half of the "Ten Wings" — the bulk of the commentaries appended to the text.

The Confucians, by and large, were not as concerned with the cosmological implications of the *I Ching* as were their contemporary Taoist "rivals." But with the possible exception of Chuang-tsu, the Taoists left little literature. The Confucians leaned more toward the sociocultural view, and they left an extensive amount of written thought behind them. The one magnificent and lasting exception to Confucian preoccupation with social concerns exists in the document (probably authored by Confucius himself) known as *Ta Chuan* (Great Treatise). This profound and very cosmic discussion of the *Book of Changes* is a virtual wellspring of intimate researches and subtle probings. We shall examine some of its comments closely in chapter eight, in which we deal with "creative mutations."

Of the post-Confucian thinkers of China, two names in particular stand out in my mind as having made a significant contribution to original thought on the *I Ching*. The first was Wang Pi (A.D. 226–49), whose treatise on the images of the *Book of Changes* influenced the direction of *I Ching* commentaries for about six or seven centuries after him — a rather extraordinary feat, considering that he died at the wise old age of twenty-three. His particular slant to the classic was toward its status as a book of wisdom, and his interest in its oracular powers was either minimal or completely immaterial.

The second name is far more important from my perspective, since it is of a man who fathered a *way* of looking at the *I Ching,* a way your author has taken up, to carry on as if it were the family jewels. This man was Shao Yung, and he worshiped the marriage of sense and number possibly even more than I do. I believe that I understand why he took this approach, though a full millennium and a whole planet lie between us. The world of the marriage of sense and number is the only possible world that could have germinated the *Book of Changes.* And when one feels about the *Book of Changes* as Shao Yung did, one is greatly impressed by such a notion.

Like the lost ancients who pioneered the *I Ching,* he grasped the basic intuition that makes the system work — the role of pure number in a universe of continuous change must necessarily lie "beyond" the normal state of affairs in matter. Perhaps this is almost another way of saying that mathematical ideas exist in and of themselves, preceding our use of them. But not quite.

One thing is for sure, however: The interlocking numerical fabric of the *I Ching,* presented through a coherent system, certainly represents one of the first attempts in the history of thought to make sense out of numbers beyond their human usefulness. Our more common notion of the idea of number leads us to suppose that we have created it to use toward our practical ends.

The reverse idea — that number has created us to serve *its* practical ends — doesn't sit so well with us for some reason. Nonetheless, number — absolute number, you see — not only exists in its own right, but is eternal as well.

The notion of a *constant,* for instance, seems to be

a good model of what I am somewhat awkwardly trying to express. It is known that the speed of the initial propagation of a light beam is a constant. Light is propagated at exactly the same rate regardless of the speed and direction of its source.

In quantum mechanics, it is also well-known that electrons have the most peculiar habit of being able to jump from orbital to orbital in atoms without in any way traversing the distance between the orbitals; they do so, furthermore, while reflecting energy potentials that are always perfect multiples of real, whole, rational numbers. We are no longer naive enough to attempt to build a physical model of this "event" — we have learned simply to accept it. Electrons obey the laws of whole numbers in some way, and that is all there is to it.

With the *I Ching,* the existence of real, whole, rational numbers is a complete universe in itself. I don't believe that even Shao Yung knew why the numbers involved in the *I Ching* work as they do — he knew only that the system would fall apart without them. By way of analogy, we might say that number functions in the *I Ching* the way the mathematics of rhythm, tonality, and harmony do in art and music. In these realms, the aesthetic extension of pure mathematical ratios can take on a magical sense for which there is no substitute.

This concern of Shao Yung's thought with the sensual-mathematical aspects of the *I Ching* led to a very curious episode in the *I Ching's* history — an episode that involved the great mathematician Leibniz, almost half a millenium after Shao Yung's death. It has been documented by quite a number of people since then, and has found Hellmut Wilhelm calling it "one of the most extraordinary episodes in the history of the human mind."

It appears that Shao Yung spent a great deal of time and energy attempting to organize the sixty-four hexagrams into a more meaningful sequence than he felt existed at that time. He was apparently aware that a number of sequences had already been devised, and he probably also knew that this had been more or less an arbitrary matter of small consequence. To this very day the sequence of the hexagrams plays virtually no role in oracle consultation.

But Shao Yung experimented and devised a very special arrangement. Laid end to end, his particular sequence of yin and yang lines constitutes a perfect mirror image of the numbers one to sixty-four expressed in the binary system of numeration worked out by Leibniz almost five hundred years later.

This is really extraordinary! Hellmut Wilhelm asks us to imagine Leibniz's excitement when Jesuit missionaries introduced him to the *I Ching* and to Shao Yung's sequence and he recognized this amazing parallel. Since Leibniz was a man who sought mathematical demonstrations of spiritual truths, we can well imagine that this discovery must have been one of the great "*eurekas*" of his life.

The present era has already witnessed the rise and celebration of a whole new generation of fresh thought in connection with the *Book of Changes.* Some ascribe the origin of this modern interest to James Legge's translation of the *I Ching* in the second half of the nineteenth century. I don't believe that this is true, though I'm sure this translation helped bring the (at that time, somewhat obscure) classic before the emerging modern world view.

But Legge's translation was significant more for its accuracy than for any philosophical orientation to our more modern view of the *I Ching.* It is important because it is *precise.* Whether he even believed in the *I Ching*'s oracular possibilities seems doubtful.

Instead, it is to Richard Wilhelm that we truly owe our gratitude. He, more than any other single person, is responsible for the interest that has been sparked in the modern eye. What he did not regenerate for us, Carl Jung and Hellmut Wilhelm did after him. I shall refer to these three men in the chapters to follow. I have taken no pains to conceal my gratitude for their efforts. Without Jung, in particular, the whole renaissance now taking place in the occult and semioccult sciences would be unimaginable.

Since I have spent most of this chapter absorbed

in the history of the *I Ching,* it is only fair that I give a bit of my personal history with the system as well. As I mentioned in the preface, I have been very fortunate in my associations with the *Book of Changes.* I have usually obtained hexagrams that make perfect sense, and even when I haven't, I have always obtained at least initially valuable ideas that led me to a suitable contemplation of my inquiry.

My first hexagram was *FELLOWSHIP WITH MEN,* and it was drawn when two close friends and I sat down to explore the *I Ching's* possibilities for the first time. The text (according to the Wilhelm-Baynes translation) for this hexagram reads:

Fellowship with men in the open.
Success.
It furthers one to cross the great water.
The perseverance of the superior man furthers.

Richard Wilhelm explains this reading as follows.

True fellowship among men must be based upon a concern that is universal. It is not the private interests of the individual that create lasting fellowship among men, but rather the goals of humanity. That is why it is said that fellowship with men in the open succeeds. If unity of this kind prevails, even difficult and dangerous tasks, such as crossing the great water, can be accomplished. But in order to bring about this sort of fellowship, a persevering and enlightened leader is needed — a man with clear, convincing, and inspiring aims and the strength to carry them out.

This was a convincingly impressive statement to us at the time, coming as it did out of a very definite "fellowship with men in the open." That fellowship was a very successful one, too. It led, for one thing, to quite a number of the ideas discussed in this work. The eventual falling away of that fellowship — fortunately, after many interesting and meaningful speculations had been shared — was due to the rise of our "private interests" as individuals and the waning of a sincere and deeply shared "concern that is universal." But the change was long overdue in each of us anyway, and the *I Ching* eventually told us that, too.

My most startling association with the *I Ching* occurred in spring 1970. I drew only eight hexagrams (for myself) all season. Six of them were the single hexagram *DELIVERANCE,* and the other two were *BITING THROUGH* and the *JOYOUS. DELIVERANCE* occurred four times in a row. The reader has no idea how this struck me at the time. I had had the unfortunate experience the autumn before of undergoing a most tragic ending to a four-year love relationship. My initial despondency had been very great, persisting well into the next year.

When it had endured to the point where I thought I might never recover from it, Leslie Shepard introduced me to the three-stringed dulcimer. The renewed enchantment that I began to find in life through this instrument was very deep.

And when I eventually realized that my life would once again be joyous and productive, I knew that I had finally recovered the ultimate drive toward the meaning of my personal existence. When I am constructing something, I am happy. When I am making music, I am happiest. My ability to make music once again was a true "deliverance."

I have never bothered to calculate the odds of obtaining a single hexagram six times out of eight. But the odds of obtaining any single hexagram twice in a row are 1 in 64. The odds of obtaining it three times consecutively are 1 in 4,096. The odds I surmounted in obtaining *DELIVERANCE* four times in a row were 1 in 262,144. As you might surmise, the text of this hexagram read like a God-given testament to me then.

After a number of years of sincere dedication to the *I Ching,* a most striking and singular truth begins to blossom in the more humble regions of one's personal soul. This blossoming grows into a lasting impression that is far easier to grasp intuitively than to convey rationally — the intuitive knowledge that one is dealing with an intelligence behind the cryptic images and archaic notions of the

I Ching. No human definition can adequately explain this intelligence. I do not necessarily mean this in what could commonly be called the religious sense, though I'm no longer at all sure what distinguishes the sacred from the secular.

I do know that I have been awed from time to time with the precision and wisdom of this intelligence. Fifty yarrow stalks and a fifty-century-old text can give meaningful answers to questions that could not even be approached by any other means; this is a startling enough matter by itself. When it is further realized that this peculiar "happening" also satisfies any conceivable definition of intelligence, one's curiosity and reverence tend to gravitate toward the most basic ponderings imaginable.

What, indeed, *is* the agent at work within the *I Ching?* The prosaic side of my nature turns toward defining the universe as a structured, interlocking fantasy of intimate relationships so accurately fixed by law that change cannot touch any one part without producing some corresponding movement in all the other parts — that is, the antithesis of the so-called absurd universe. But this is the prosaic side of my opinion. It will be explored in the next chapter under the notion of *synchronicity.*

The poetic side of me inclines itself toward a new definition of life or intelligence altogether. If human conscious existence is as the biologists, geologists, psychologists, and astrophysicists say it is — the product of several billion years of incredible material processes, culminating in a movement toward self-awareness – I am struck by the thought of what all our molten lava must have meant to begin with. What is there in hot rocks that already possesses every possible seed of things to come?

Whatever happens to be within us – and therefore in the earth that has so magically conjured us up – certainly stretches its imagination to the limits in trying to find itself. Unless one is of the persuasion that something can come from nothing, one is left with a universe that contains, has always contained, and always will contain life and not only life, but intelligence, as well.

After all, intelligent beings are composed of the same old protons, neutrons, and electrons that form the building blocks of material existence. To say that one arrangement of them is "intelligent and alive" and another "dumb and dead" makes about as much sense to me as to say that wholly different arrangements of Tinker Toys produce entirely different qualities in themselves.

I am left with the lingering feeling that the *I Ching* is a celebration of eternal life – not the eternal life of my or anyone else's body or mind, but the eternal fount of life that is the universe's infinite and omnipresent birthright. But let us get back to the prosaics at hand and question the actual operations of the *I Ching* more closely.

'There is one common flow . . .
all things are in sympathy.'
hippocrates

CHAPTER THREE

The Principle of Synchronicity

There is one common flow, one common breathing, all things are in sympathy. The whole organism and each one of its parts are working in conjunction for the same purpose . . . the great principle extends to the extremest part, and from the extremest part it returns to the great principle, to the one nature, being and not-being.

— Hippocrates, *De alimento*

Since its formal introduction into the mainstream of modern Western thought by Carl Jung nearly forty years ago, the *principle of synchronicity* has come of age. It has spun out of itself such a convincing web of reason and respectability that even the most dedicated empiricists are beginning to have second and third thoughts about it. The principle is essentially rational and testable, and experiments conducted all over the world since Jung's first famous experiment in astrology have nearly always spoken quite favorably for it.

Before the synchronicity principle, mystic research—astrology in particular—was continually burdened with having to explain how any meaningful connection could exist between two seemingly remote events. That the sun and moon might in some way affect the course of human affairs was never too preposterous a claim. Astrologers could point to such things as tidal and climate changes and allow their arguments to proceed somewhat plausibly, if awkwardly, from there. But to claim that the constellation Scorpius ascending on the horizon at a person's birth would have a great deal to do with the growth of that person's character was quite another story indeed. Sophisticated astrologers were often no happier than their skeptical critics at having to conjure up everything from "God's omnipotence" to "higher forms of energy" to attempt to explain this ultimate mystery of their science. And this "influence" theory became less and less credible as we began to acquire a greater feel for the immensity of cosmic distances.

The synchronicity principle came about just in time to save our little show. There is nothing inordinately complicated about the idea behind this principle, though it does take some time for cause-oriented minds to adjust to it. Carl Jung in *Synchronicity: An Acausal Connecting Principle* calls it the "acausal connecting principle," defining it in contrast to the law of causality as follows.

> This . . . involves a certain curious principle that I have termed synchronicity, a concept that formulates a point of view diametrically opposed to that of causality. Since the latter is a merely statistical truth and not absolute, it is a sort of working hypothesis of how events evolve one out of another, whereas synchronicity takes the coincidence of events in space and time as meaning something more than mere chance, namely, a peculiar interdependence of objective events among themselves as well as with the subjective (psychic) states of the observer or observers.

This is not so mystical as it might at first appear. Suppose that we have an enormous machine composed of hundreds of cogs, lights, bells, wheels, buzzers, and whatever. Now, so long as all these parts are connected in some way — *either physically or by rate equations* — observing any one part at a particular time would enable us to predict the state of any other part. Note that I said that this relation-

ship can be either physical or mathematical, because causality and synchronicity are the principles
that correspond to those notions. Systems like the *I
Ching* and astrology are simply more ambitious
assertions of this same model. Something "out
there" corresponds to something "in here" because
both events exist in the same universe, obey all the
same laws, and most probably even had a common
origin.

If the synchronicity principle seems to fall back on
both the space-time continuum of the general theory
of relativity and the "big bang" theory of cosmoge-
nesis, that is all the more to its credit — both of those
theories are gathering more supporting evidence
with time. But strictly speaking, synchronicity need
not coincide with these theories. That it stands even
as a postulate — a collective first postulate for all the
mystic sciences–is good enough for now. The best
that we can offer as "proof" for this principle is to
point to experimentation done in the sciences based
on this principle (like Jung's astrology experiment).
Such experimentation has been very successful.

Since I have mentioned the connection of synchronicity with the better-known theories of mainstream physics, I shall mention other parallels as
well. The phenomenon of radioactive decay has been
particularly baffling from the causal viewpoint. The
spontaneous disintegration of certain atoms
through radioactive emission is an event for which

modern physics cannot provide an answer of suitable notion and image. But it is quite in keeping with a synchronistic view of things. No less a figure than the physicist Sir James Jeans says of this mystery, "Radioactive break-up appeared to be an effect without a cause, and suggested that the ultimate laws of nature were not even causal."

If we add to the radioactivity puzzle such related puzzles as are found in the quantum theory, Heisenberg's uncertainty principle, and most of the tenets cited in Einstein's general theory of relativity, an impressive case can be made for incorporating the synchronicity principle into mainstream physics.

When the unified field theory is worked out to the bone — the evidence here, too, is mounting steadily — and the entire clockworks of the cosmos can be brought under a set of unifying equations, this will be the final touch for bringing the synchronicity principle into full popularity among scientists.

Really expert gamblers know better than most people that odds are seldom as regular as probability theory would have us believe. They would find Confucius in their company if they attempted to make a law of their findings. Probability theory states that if you throw a coin fifty times, it will most probably turn up heads twenty-five times and tails twenty-five times, and the more tosses are made, the more likely the distribution will be fifty-fifty.

Actually, this is nearly the opposite of the truth. Very rarely will the tosser end up with an equal number of heads and tails, and the *more* tosses are made, the less chance there is of equality. A few minutes of experimentation can verify this simple observation. Now, this does not mean that we must throw probability theory out the window. For most cases to which it is applied it works very well. It always works well when only an *approximation* of values is required. Where precision of the first rank is required, one is left having to account for an endless number of small discrepancies.

I maintain that these small discrepancies are part and parcel of divination. In the *I Ching's* view, these deviations are responsible for differences in the whole spectrum of observable phenomena. Among the network of living beings, in general, and of human situations, in particular, these deviations from the probable separate and distinguish the qualities of living existence. Coupled with this idea is the further implication that the improbable will triumph in the long run, however rare it appears against the greater background of the probable. This is no more difficult to grasp than it has been to recognize what modern science already understands of life — that the evolution of continually more complex organisms has occurred in direct opposition to the more probable and natural trend of matter (and energy) to dissipate into more and more simple forms.

It makes little difference whether life has some kind of internal driving force that makes the exception or is, instead, simply the one-in-a-billion occurrence that must also have its day. It's beside the point entirely. It matters only that we understand the importance of minute deviations in nature and realize that our very existence is some sort of a triumph for the improbable.

The *I Ching* has been created in the image of life. It sustains itself in the spirit of life. Whatever deviations were accountable for the origin and ascent of our kind of consciousness, these deviations were recognized and built into the very guts of the *I Ching's* procedure. That is, the hexagram is man's special equation for recognizing a synchronistic sympathy between himself and his world.

But perhaps synchronicity is not enough. I have often wondered what synchronicity had to do with the person performing the divination. If it were simply a matter of seeing the fall of the yarrow stalks as the physical-mathematical counterpoint of a force in the unconscious at the moment of divination, then we must ask, how do I know that this is *my* hexagram? How do I know that it is not someone else's? More exactly, how can I divine my own hexagram, as well as divine someone else's at the mere flip of a switch in my *intentions?*

Good question. Obviously, not everyone has the same hexagram at the same time—certainly not the same advice could be offered to everyone in the world simultaneously. So we must look deeper. It is a matter of *intending* your synchronicity or my synchronicity or another person's synchronicity during the process of divination. But I don't have even the faintest idea of what it means to say "my synchronicity."

This problem has led many to use parapsychology to seek out the basis of the *I Ching's* oracular powers. Although this is perhaps not a bad idea, the people who do this do it more in skeptical reservation than in a spirit of true inquiry. It is extremely interesting to me that some people feel that they are being conservative now when claiming that something is due only to ESP!

How things have changed. Now that ESP has been scientifically proved in the laboratory, it too can be considered as a good weapon to use against more esoteric approaches. *But what is behind ESP?*

I think that those who resort to ESP as the conservative explanation of these issues are doing so because they find it easier to visualize some obscure "transmission of energy" than to imagine something as "radical" as a universal sympathy of events. But as a clear matter of fact, no category of psi phenomena has ever been proved to be a transmission of any type of energy; in fact, the evidence seems to show that it is anything but that. To assume that energy is involved in ESP phenomena, we must postulate an energy faster than light, impervious to any energy field we know of, and totally independent of all space-time considerations. I find this hypothesis far more fantastic and unbelievable than synchronicity.

Under such assumptions, for instance, how could precognition be explained? How can that which has not yet happened transmit an energy to the present? But synchronicity handles the explanation only to well. Thinking back to the machine model I gave earlier in the chapter, it is clear that we could predict the future of any part based on the present state of any other part, knowing the equations that unite them. For the time being, I feel it would be wise for us to follow one of the cardinal rules of science — side with the simpler solution until it becomes necessary to overhaul one's whole world view.

I am still back to the problem of what to do about *my* synchronicity — especially if ESP, too, might be synchronistic. I can only say that in some manner, my unconscious has willed a particular orientation of the synchronicity process. But how can the unconscious "will"?

What can probably be concluded after all is said is that we either simply don't know enough about these realms of phenomena or don't yet have adequate definitions for the terms we are applying to them. But this will hardly make most of us shy. We will still partake of the *I Ching's* universe with the good conscience of knowing that it continues to be more than all that we can *say* of it. The hows and whys behind this great and mysterious system will remain interesting points to ponder in more idle moments. Our real work will be immersed in its execution.

DIVINING . . . BY NOTING THE PATH OF A GOLDFISH
AS IT SWIMS THROUGH SIXTEEN PORTALS

PART TWO

**

TECHNICAL RELATIONS
AMONG
HEXAGRAMS

CHAPTER FOUR

The Nuclear Concept
of Change

Since even the novice is aware that the system of the
I Ching is rooted very firmly in the realm of number
and numerical sequence, it is surprising that this
aspect has been so largely unexplored or under-
emphasized. For however profoundly the text of the
Book of Changes enters into the highest faculties of
human consciousness and unconsciousness, it must
never be forgotten that the *I Ching* is a child born of
rigidly basic, mathematical parentage. The hexagram was created out of the play of the yin and the
yang through the realm of numerical relation, and it

is to this play that we must offer our gratitude for the results.

No one knows how the yarrow-stalk system came about. All that is reasonably known is that the system must have grown up fairly closely with the text and that this method is far older and certainly more soundly based than some of the sister systems, such as the coin method, the six-wands method, and so forth (see Appendix A).

I should make it clear that this excludes the ancient bone oracle, which led to the yarrow-stalk method. Apparently the bone oracle was the first method by which the *I Ching* could be consulted in an oracular fashion, but it was not really the *I Ching* at all in those days. The bone oracle was used only to answer questions of the yes-or-no variety. When the question was posed, a bone was placed into a fire and allowed to crack. If the crack crossed over the whole cross-section of the bone, the answer was regarded as yang (yes). If the bone cracked on both sides of the ridge — that is, if the heat wasn't sufficient to form a crack crossing the whole curve of the bone — the answer was regarded as yin (no). This seems to be the oldest surviving evidence of anything remotely connected to the *I Ching* system.

By the time of King Wên and the Duke of Chou (thirteenth century B.C.), the *I Ching* had evolved into a sophisticated text with an accompanying system of divination probably little different from our present method of dividing the yarrow stalks.

Each step in the yarrow-stalk method can be seen to have a meaningful connotation in its mechanics which stretches back to its original relationships to nature during the formative years of its creation. Chapter nine, section three, Wilhelm/Baynes translation, pages 310, 311 in the *Ta Chuan* of Confucius says,

> The number of the total is fifty. Of these, forty-nine are used. They are divided into two portions, to represent the two primal forces. Hereupon one is set apart, to represent the three powers. They are counted through by fours, to represent the four seasons. The remainder is put aside, to represent the intercalary month. There are two intercalary months in five years, therefore the putting aside is repeated, and this gives us the whole.

And Richard Wilhelm says of this process:

> Here the process of consulting the oracle is brought into relation with cosmic processes.

If this is indeed *the* method of doing the *I Ching* — the oldest, wisest, most traditional — my question is simply, is there anything inherent in the divination process that could lead us to a greater understanding of the *I Ching* as a whole?

It was not inspiration that led me deep within the numerical world of the *I Ching*. It was, rather, simply a curiosity about certain peculiarities I noticed in divining hexagrams over a long period of time. To begin with, I observed that certain hexagrams occurred quite often, for all kinds of people in all kinds of situations, while many others occurred rarely or not at all. I have got particular hexagrams literally dozens of times, while I haven't even come close to getting certain others.

Assuming that divining several hundred hexagrams over a long period of time (again, for quite a multitude of people and situations) should produce a fairly equal distribution over the sixty-four possibilities, I became curious enough to explore this peculiarity. It eventually dawned on me that it was not exactly hexagrams that were being distributed unequally, but the lines themselves. I found that to be even weirder. One would naturally think that the lines of the hexagrams would be far more evenly distributed than the hexagrams, but that wasn't true. The hexagrams occurred unequally only because the lines did.

A more detailed observation was even more incredible — the unchanging female line was by far the most common occurrence in divination. Now, if the universe was supposedly balanced between the yin and the yang forces, as the *Book of Changes* would at first have us believe, what unusual agent would make it seem otherwise here?

I considered a number of hypothetical ideas at first, but none bore themselves out convincingly enough. The unbalanced distribution of lines did not distinguish themselves from the basic pattern whether the hexagram was done for me or for someone else, for man or for woman, to seek out a mundane answer to a mundane situation or to pursue the most general and basic universal truths. What's more, it was becoming apparent that the female *changing* line was the line of least occurrence.

Richard Wilhelm left me the clue to solving this important puzzle. In the appendix of his translation dealing with the yarrow-stalk divining method, he says that the first division of the stalks can produce a nine in one way and a five in three different ways. The two divisions after the first one are then equally divided between obtaining an eight or a four.

I satisfied myself with this claim by counting the forty-nine stalks out through enough of their possible divisions to see the pattern myself. Since it was obvious that any line beginning with five stalks on the first count would be three times more likely to occur than those which began with a nine, it was easy enough after that to construct the following table showing the relative probabilities of the four possible lines.

Yin changing	(-X-)	1 out of 16 times
Yang changing	(-θ-)	3 out of 16 times
Yang unchanging	(——)	5 out of 16 times
Yin unchanging	(- -)	7 out of 16 times

A whole tidal wave of implications swept over me after this discovery. The first important implication was that this showed the coin method to be empirically wrong. The ratio of the lines in the stalk method is one-three-five-seven. The coins reflect the respective ratios of two-two-six-six. That is, the coins make no distinction between the two unchanging or the two changing lines, as the yarrow-stalk method does.

Nearly a year after this personal discovery I encountered further confirmation of it in an article written by Hellmut Wilhelm more than two decades ago. In "The Concept of Time in the *Book of Changes*," from the *Eranos Notebooks,* Wilhelm states,

> But a further probability is incorporated in this method, namely that rest and change are diversely divided between yin and yang, so that yang is more inclined (3:5) toward change than is the yin (1:7).

At this writing a further reference to those ratios has appeared in the January 1974 issue of *Scientific American.* Martin Gardner says,

> The probability that a broken line will change is $1/16$ as compared to $3/16$ for an unbroken line (or respective probabilities of $7/16$ versus $5/16$ that the lines will remain stable). In other words, when sticks are cast, it is three times more likely that an unbroken line will change than a broken one.

80

As far as the relationship of the stalk method to the coin method is concerned, he gives my view above further support.

> Purists who object to coin-casting have sound mathematical support. Not only does the stick ritual discourage frivolous consultation but also its asymmetry produces a more interesting set of probabilities.

As far as I know, Wilhelm did not realize the full implication of these ratios. At least, he never wrote further about it. Besides the simple observation that the coins do not reflect the basic ratios, there are tremendous implications for the *I Ching* as a whole.

To begin with, the hexagram takes on a brand new perspective. If certain lines are more probable than others, then it follows that certain hexagrams are also more probable. Hexagrams are, after all, simply sixfold accumulations of individual lines. This notion leads us to the even more astounding conclusion that the ancient Chinese had some kind of grasp of what we now call *entropy*. The fact that a male (strong) line tends to break apart more easily than a female (weak) line will build up is a clear exposition of the entropy principle. Another way of saying this is to state that the universe tends more toward the receptive than it does toward the creative. In fact, it does so about eight times more readily.

It is incredible enough that the second law of thermodynamics was grasped intuitively perhaps as long as thirty centuries ago. That it was pragmatically applied to human life through the sixty-four hexagrams is still more incredible. But before going on to a more detailed discussion of how this new understanding can be applied to the relationships among the hexagrams, let me digress a moment to discuss the full meaning of this concept as it applies to divination methods.

I had an aesthetic aversion to the coin method long before I came to understand its empirical errors. It is a "lazy man's method," condensing the twenty-minute yarrow-stalk operation into about one minute. But ironically enough, this new understanding of the ratios inherent in the yarrow-stalk method allows for an even "lazier" method. Since the fundamental ratios are based on relative sections of the number sixteen, I call it the sixteen system. It is as empirically correct as the stalk method but is much faster than even the coin method.

At its simplest manual level, all that is required is sixteen colored beads. These beads (or sticks, buttons, pebbles, and so on) are in four different hues, reflecting the ratio one-three-five-seven. As the diviner meditates on the question, he or she mixes the beads (which are hidden from view) and picks one. If, for instance, the color drawn is represented three times in the sixteen beads, the bead represents a male changing line.

There is not the slightest numerical difference between this drawing of a single bead and the threefold separation of the stalks. The difference is purely aesthetic. For very important questions, I still use the stalk method. I enjoy the time it takes to obtain a hexagram in that manner. But for concerns that require divining several hexagrams, this sixteen system has proved very useful and effective. Its one great advantage is that the hexagram drawn is more truly a reflection of a single moment. Also, it is much easier for most people to remain fully attentive to the question at hand for twenty seconds than to endure the countless distractions (both internal and external) that tend to pollute or disrupt the meditation of twenty minutes.

As a practical suggestion I would also urge the student experimenting with this new method to use more than sixteen beads. As long as the one-three-five-seven ratio is maintained in the coloring, any multiple of sixteen beads is possible. I advise it only because it makes for easier mixing of the beads — just as it is easier to shuffle fifty cards than ten.

It is possible to achieve even faster, more "efficient" means of divining. If an ideal is to be made out of wedding the divination time as closely as possible to the moment of pure inquiry, then we now have the means to do so through the advancements of computer science. By the use of a computer designed on the sixteen system (see Appendix C), a hexagram can be obtained in far less than one second!

Almost anyone could build a more practical mechanical model at very little cost. It would consist simply of six wheels, each with sixteen indentations or protrusions marked in some way to reflect the basic ratios. The six wheels could be given a hard spin manually and then stopped at random with the finger, one after the other. This is essentially the same idea as would be used by the computer. The main difference is that a computer would use binary counters in place of wheels.

Actually, the possibilities are limited only by the imagination. One imaginative colleague even suggested noting the path of a goldfish as it swims back and forth through a wall with sixteen marked portals! Why not? Or how about creating the *slowest* method by having sixteen turtles "race" to a finish line six times! After all, according to some legends, the *I Ching* began with tortoise shells — why not have it end with the whole tortoise?

Jesting and mechanics aside, let me come back to the issue at hand. It is not at all important that the student adopt any of these new methods — my suggestions are offered more in a spirit of fun or experimentation than anything else. The student who wishes to stick with the yarrow-stalk method certainly has my complete blessing. I would hope that students will believe me, however, when I claim that the sixteen system does work. The private researches my friends and I have done with it seem fully positive.

What is far more at issue is not the method, but the meaning, of the *I Ching* system. What do the basic ratios mean to the system as a whole? What is the universal difference between one hexagram and another? For these answers, we must take a slightly longer stride into the Changes.

The Creative and the Receptive

CHAPTER FIVE

Primary and Secondary Relationships

In his recent brilliant thesis on the *I Ching*, Professor Jung Young Lee pointed out that the hexagram has the same relationship to life as the atom does to chemistry. Both are the building blocks of their universes, and both have the possibility of transforming themselves or being transformed into others of their kind. My question for the moment is, are the hexagrams linked by bonds as tightly woven as the elements of the periodic table?

The answer is a most definite yes. I hinted at it in the last chapter, and now we shall take it out by the roots and examine it.

If the lines of a hexagram are taken one at a time, the probabilities represented by a whole hexagram would simply be the multiplication of the probabilities of each line. The *CREATIVE* would simply be the least probable hexagram and the *RECEPTIVE* the most probable, with the other sixty-two falling somewhere between. But it is not quite that simple.

Not only the probabilities of individual lines, but also the various permutations in which they may be found are involved. It is true, for instance, that the *RECEPTIVE,* with no changing lines, is made up of the six most probable lines. But that occurrence itself (six female lines in a row) adds a further factor, suggesting a somewhat unlikely arrangement. A hexagram with six female lines occurs only once in the *Book of Changes.* A hexagram with only five female and one male may be "tainted" with the single yang line, but there are six possible hexagrams with that arrangement. Likewise, there are fifteen hexagrams with four yin and two yang lines, and so on.

The *total* likelihood of any stable hexagram's occurring in a single divination is represented by the following equation.

$$Hp = N(7/16^f \times 5/16^m)$$

Hp represents the total probability of the hexagram.

N represents the number of times that the particular distribution (like four yin–two yang, three yin–three yang, and so on) occurs in the total sixty-four. *F* stands for the number of female lines in the hexagram; *M*, the number of male. It should be clearly understood that changing lines do not enter into this picture at all. For the time being, we are interested only in the relationships among stable hexagrams.

Using the above equation, I undertook the calculations necessary (see Appendix B) and arrived at the Periodic Table of the Sixty-four Hexagrams.

Let us explore some of the more important uses of this chart. Generally, the chart moves from top to bottom in order of increasing probability. If the diviner obtains a hexagram in the lower part of the chart, the hexagram is a very likely one. *If the diviner so wishes,* he or she can more probably maintain this state of affairs with less energy and commitment than if the hexagram were higher in the chart.

As one moves upward in the chart, one encounters hexagrams of an increasingly unstable nature. The *CREATIVE* is the most unstable condition of all and is therefore the most difficult to maintain.

The *CREATIVE,* like hydrogen among the chemical elements, is the basic unit of the periodic series. I have given its unit probability as one "yangstrom." This measure is relative and has meaning only

Periodic Table

of the

Sixty-Four Hexagrams

Group	Type	Y°	Hexagram Numbers
I	6 Yang	1	1
II	6 Yin	7.5	2
III	1 Yin 5 Yang	8.5	9 10 13 14 43 44
IV	2 Yin 4 Yang	29.5	5 6 25 26 28 30 33 34 37 38 49 50 57 58 61
V	5 Yin 1 Yang	32.5	7 8 15 16 23 24
VI	3 Yin 3 Yang	55	11 12 17 18 21 22 31 32 41 42 47 48 53 54 55 56 59 60 63 64
VII	4 Yin 2 Yang	56.5	3 4 19 20 27 29 35 36 39 40 45 46 51 52 62

when it is involved with the connections among stable hexagrams.

If the student were to obtain, for example, the hexagram called *STANDSTILL,* she or he could tell from the chart how far more likely that state of affairs is than the *CREATIVE. STANDSTILL* falls in Group VI, the group of hexagrams that are fifty-five times more likely than the *CREATIVE.*

For convenience, it is useful to round off the probability units. Groups II and III are approximately 8 times more probable than the *CREATIVE.* Groups IV and V are about 32 times more likely than the *CREATIVE* (and 4 times more so than Groups II and III). Groups VI and VII are 56 times more common than the *CREATIVE* (7 times more so than Groups II and III and 1.75 times more than Groups IV and V).

These unit quantities should not, as far as I can tell, be used as quantitative absolutes in matters of comparison. They are more important insofar as they are able to give the diviner a feeling for where he or she stands at the time. The higher up the chart the hexagram is, the more energy and discipline will be needed to keep the situation together.

These value judgments can be applied in reverse, as well. If one obtains a "negative" hexagram at the top of the chart, one will have less difficulty dissipating it than if it had occurred at the bottom. A "negative" hexagram from the bottom of the chart will require far more work to alleviate, since it has an inherent and natural tendency to persist.

Take a look at the hexagram called *POSSESSION IN GREAT MEASURE* (14). This hexagram indicates a situation of great wealth, financial or otherwise. It occurs in Group III, a very unstable group. True, it is eight times stronger and more probable than The *CREATIVE,* but it is also seven times weaker and more rare than the thirty-five hexagrams in Groups VI and VII, which constitute more than half of all possible hexagrams. Conclusion: it will require a good deal of energy to maintain *POSSESSION IN GREAT MEASURE.*

An interesting relationship exists between the *CREATIVE* and the *RECEPTIVE.* The *RECEPTIVE* represents the rarest state in the Changes except for the *CREATIVE;* yet it is still 7.529536 times more probable. That figure, quite peculiarly, happens to be exact. In some way or another, it reflects a ratio that seems to be a universal constant in the *I Ching's* version of the universe.

This is puzzling since we know very well that the cosmos ought to maintain a perfectly equal balance of the yin and yang forces. The whole foundation of the *I Ching* stems from that idea. The only way around the discrepancy lies in the possibility that the sphere of living systems (which the *Book of Changes* represents for the human realm) is inclined more to the yin, with the difference in the balance being made up elsewhere.

This is an amazing idea. In terms of percentages, this universal ratio means that any single living system or event will most likely be diversely divided between the yin and yang as follows: 88 percent yin, 12 percent yang. That is, in terms of entropy, about 88 percent tends toward the greater probability of disintegrating into the equilibrium of the *RECEPTIVE,* and 12 percent tends toward the lesser probability of growing and expanding with the *CREATIVE.*

Let me suggest a cosmic possibility behind this issue. If we assume that the sun is 100 percent yang (not a farfetched assumption) and that the space into which it pours is 100 percent yin, we can see that anything between them will be of some mixture. Our ratio suggests that at a certain point in evolution, the division will eventually turn up as 88 percent yin, 12 percent yang, and that is the type of existence that we are now actualizing. The *Book of Changes* was written out of and for this particular balance.

Now, I'm not entirely sure that these ideas stemming from a comparison of the *CREATIVE* and the *RECEPTIVE* mean exactly what I have conjectured they mean. It is pure guesswork, and I know it. But this is really not so important as what is actually found within the hexagrams as a whole. I have merely taken this tangent to demonstrate one meditational possibility arising from the Periodic Table.

The Periodic Table *is* important and valid, and I hope others will make as much good use of it as I have.

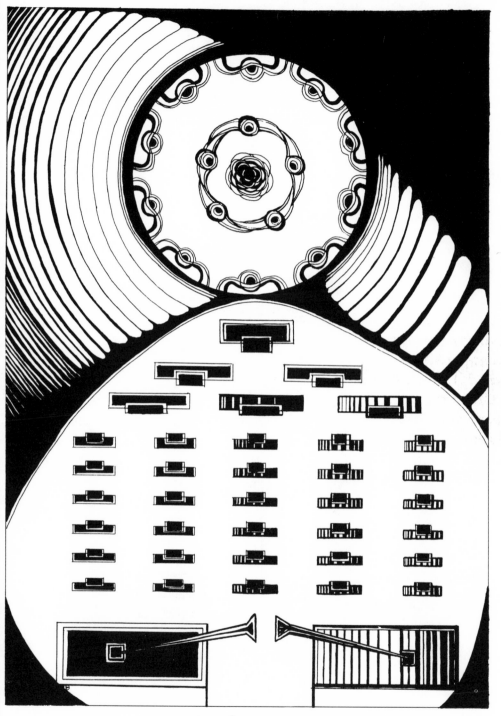

a pair of antigrams:
fellowship with men versus the army

CHAPTER SIX

Hexagram Families

Let us push the Periodic Table to the back of our thoughts for a moment and examine a number of other ideas that arise independently. We shall return to the Periodic Table later.

The *CREATIVE* and the *RECEPTIVE* are exact opposites in meaning as well as in structure; this made me wonder about polarity among the hexagrams in general. Since the *I Ching* calls these two parent hexagrams the two primal ingredients from which the other sixty-two hexagrams are derived, I wonder how far one can go in holding them up as examples. Specifically, do structurally opposite hexagrams–henceforth called *antigrams*–exhibit opposite meanings as well? If the *CREATIVE* and the *RECEPTIVE* can be held up as an example, I believe that we can give our answer in the affirmative, but first let us explore the notion more deeply.

It is clear that a hexagram with all six lines changing represents a situation of extreme instability. But what does this mean? It means, first of all, that the hexagram has been polarized to the maximum degree in its structure. Second, if the trauma of this mutation is to have any significance at all, the significance will have to lie in a polarization of meaning as well as in structure.

Quite frequently, the serious student of the Changes is confronted with a dilemma of translation. One translation of the *Book of Changes* calls a hexagram one thing, and another calls it something else. Usually this is no great matter. Richard Wilhelm calls the third hexagram *DIFFICULTY AT THE BEGINNING,* and another translator calls it *BIRTH PAINS.* That's not too bad. But when Wilhelm calls the sixteenth hexagram *ENTHUSIASM,* and John Blofeld calls it *REPOSE,* that is very hard to reconcile.

An examination of the antigram can help resolve such issues. Much of the difficulty arising from divergent translations of hexagrams originates because no one can be precisely sure how certain ancient Chinese characters are to be translated or transliterated. The student is concerned not so much with what to call it, though, as with what she or he ought to *feel* about it. At the very least, meditations on the antigrams can help one to arrive at the meanings behind their correlative hexagrams.

A hexagram, as I've said, relates to its antigram through the great void of six lines changing. Let us look at some cases of this ultimately polar arrangement.

The *CREATIVE* and the *RECEPTIVE* are transparently obvious. Six yang and six yin. A condition of expanding creativeness contrasted to contracting receptiveness.

Many other pairs are fairly obvious too. *APPROACH* (19) and *RETREAT* (33) are antigrams whose meaning is as clearly apparent as their structural polarity. Likewise, *BEFORE COMPLETION* (64) and *AFTER COMPLETION* (63) follow the pattern.

In still other pairs, the polarity is not immediately obvious but can be found with little trouble. For instance, *THE ARMY* (7) and *FELLOWSHIP WITH MEN* (13) make interesting antigrams. Both have to do with men grouped together in a social arrangement (every pair of antigrams, I should add, are poles of a common note). But *THE ARMY* has men grouped together in an aristocratic hierarchy, and *FELLOWSHIP WITH MEN* in a cooperative, democratic order.

Another example of this type might be found in

the antigrams *YOUTHFUL FOLLY* (4) and *REVOLUTION* (49). Both have a common motif of rebellion, but the one is frivolous and disjointed, whereas the other is deep and calculated.

Many pairs, however, do not lend themselves so readily to comparison. These make for the most intriguing meditations.

Why, for instance, are hexagrams 37, *THE FAMILY,* and 40, *DELIVERANCE,* antigrams? Why doesn't *THE FAMILY* provide the ultimate release from tension that *DELIVERANCE* signifies in its textual judgment? The text of *THE FAMILY* says, "Perseverance of the woman furthers." Why is that the opposite of *DELIVERANCE?* The only answer I can suggest from my own meditations might be found in the story of the Buddha. Siddhartha had to leave his family in order to find his kind of deliverance. I'm not sure why or if this is a correct reference for these antigrams. There is a ring of truth to it for me, though I've yet to understand the implications. As you can see, there is at least enough in it to make for a good meditation.

Another way of approaching the interpretation of a hexagram is by noting its corresponding *paragram.* The paragram is the hexagram one would have received had the last line fallen the opposite way.

Contrary to the antigram, the paragram's meaning should be closely allied with that of the hexagram.

In the divination of any hexagram, the process of divination occurs in the construction of that hexagram as follows.

Line 6 eliminates only one last possibility—the paragram (totaling 63 rejections).

Line 5 eliminates 2 more (totaling 62).

Line 4 eliminates 4 more (totaling 60).

Line 3, establishing the first trigram, eliminates 8 more hexagrams (totaling 56).

Line 2 eliminates 16 (totaling 48).

Line 1 eliminates 32 of the hexagrams.

If we picture this process as a converging cone, it is easy to see that the paragram has an important significance — three complete separations of the stalks are needed to distinguish it from the hexagram finally received.

Like the antigram, the paragram can be most effectively used in trying to intuit the full meaning of the hexagram.

A table of both the antigrams and paragrams appears on the following page.

To return to the discussion of antigrams for a moment, let me mention that it is curious to observe how certain antigram pairs contrast in their probability of occurrence. Aside from the twenty hexa-

New Directions in the I Ching

Hexagram/Antigram/Paragram

Table

H	A	P
1	2	43
2	1	23
3	50	42
4	49	7
5	35	9
6	36	47
7	13	4
8	14	20
9	16	5
10	15	58
11	12	26
12	11	45
13	7	49
14	8	34
15	10	52
16	9	35
17	18	25
18	17	46
19	33	41
20	34	8
21	48	51
22	47	36
23	43	2
24	44	27
25	46	17
26	45	11
27	28	24
28	27	44
29	30	59
30	29	55
31	41	33
32	42	50
33	19	31
34	20	14
35	5	16
36	6	22
37	40	63
38	39	54
39	38	53
40	37	64
41	31	19
42	32	3
43	23	1
44	24	28
45	26	12

H	A	P
46	25	18
47	22	6
48	21	57
49	4	13
50	3	32
51	57	21
52	58	15
53	54	39
54	53	38
55	59	30
56	60	62
57	51	48
58	52	10
59	55	29
60	56	61
61	62	60
62	61	56
63	64	37
64	63	40

Example:

H	A	P
1	2	43

grams that comprise Group VI of the Periodic Table (those of three yin and three yang lines), all antigram pairs reflect divergent probability ratios. This means simply that one pole represents the more likely and the other the less likely of human situations woven around that particular common theme.

The *CREATIVE* (Group 1) and the *RECEPTIVE* (Group II) have already been discussed. The hexagrams of Group III are the less probable poles of their antigrams in Group V (with odds of about 1 to 4). Group IV hexagrams are the less probable poles of their antigrams in Group VII (1 in 2).

One good example will suffice to show what a meditational wellspring this opens up. I mentioned that *FELLOWSHIP WITH MEN* contrasts with its antigram, *THE ARMY,* in the sense that one refers to a democracy and the other to a pecking order. Looking at the Periodic Table, one sees that *THE ARMY* is the more likely state of affairs among men — in fact, it is about four times more likely, according to the *I Ching*. This may be a little too generous, as history shows, but I feel that at least the point is well made.

Closely associated with the idea of the paragram is the idea of *first families*.

The first family of the hexagram is comprised of the six hexagrams that would arise if each (but only one) of the lines of that hexagram changed. The

105

paragram is always, of course, one of those six hexagrams (the top line changing). I don't believe that any of the five family hexagrams other than the paragram can be said to be as important as the paragram unless that line is in rulership position (usually indicated in most translations by a square or a circle placed next to the line). However, all six do represent a unique place in their stand with the original hexagram, since each of them can be reached by only one organic transformation. All other hexagrams could be reached by not fewer than two nor more than six transformations. With six full changes, one would arrive, of course, at the anti-gram.

The second family would be all those hexagrams which can be reached by two transformations; the third, by three, and so on.

The full utilization of hexagram families will be discussed in the last chapter.

Before closing this section on technical relations, I would like to reveal something for which I do not yet have a good explanation. It does signify another "technical relation," even if we cannot, for the moment, figure out what it means or how we might use it.

When I discussed Shao Yung's interest in finding the "correct" sequence of the sixty-four hexagrams, I failed to mention that the sequence in use today seems to be entirely without rhyme or reason. This may not be so — at least, it may not be completely so. When simply playing around with various sequences, I encountered a very strange peculiarity. It is strange because it seems to hint at the significance of the present sequence — a significance one would not have immediately predicted.

I decided to start with the *CREATIVE,* since it is the first hexagram. I followed it up with its antigram, the *RECEPTIVE,* the second hexagram in the modern sequence. I then proceeded to hexagram 3, *DIFFICULTY AT THE BEGINNING,* and followed it up with its antigram, *THE CAULDRON* (50). Then I returned to the fourth hexagram and did likewise. I returned each time to the earliest hexagram in the sequence that had not yet been exhausted as an antigram, until all sixty-four hexagrams had been used.

The following, seemingly irrational sequence was,

1, 2, 3, 50, 4, 49, 5, 35, 6, 36, 7, 13, 8, 14, 9, 16, 10, 15, 11, 12, 17, 18, 19, 33, 20, 34, 21, 48, 22, 47, 23, 43, 24, 44, 25, 46, 26, 45, 27, 28, 29, 30, 31, 41, 32, 42, 37, 40, 38, 39, 51, 57, 52, 58, 53, 54, 55, 59, 56, 60, 61, 62, 63, 64.

Then I decided to record the sequence of *leaps* between the hexagrams and their antigrams and to note them in the same serial order. I obtained the following pattern (I am intentionally grouping them the way they appear here to make my next point).

1   47•45   30•30   6•6   7•5   1•1   14•14   27•25
20•20   21•19   1•1   10•10   3•1   6•6   1   4•4   1•1

Aside from the two isolated leaps of 1, a pattern of pairs is suggested that, aside from the small deviations, seems to constitute some sort of an ordered mathematical series. There's definitely something in the air about this series, but I can't quite identify it. It has all the odor of a perfect numerical sequence that has grown a bit polluted in the dregs of history. If someone can find a way of ironing out the bugs in this series, I would very much like to see the sequence of hexagrams as they would have to follow each other to reflect that series.

Now, let's journey to the freer but stranger land of free relations. The free relations among hexagrams are the ultimate fulfillment of their technical origins.

Destiny and the I Ching:
moving lines serve to suggest paths of travel

PART THREE

*   *

FREE RELATIONS
AMONG
HEXAGRAMS

CHAPTER SEVEN

Freedom and the Moving Line

Up to now, we have been dealing with the *I Ching* from the standpoint of what could be extracted from its mathematical nature. In these two chapters, I wish to engage us in certain intuitive possibilities that might add an entirely different dimension to approaching the *Book of Changes.*

I have avoided discussing the meaning of the changing line until now for a very important reason. The moving line, unlike the stable line, introduces to the *I Ching* a new aspect that changes its tone completely. Instead of telling you where you are, the moving line indicates where you are going. More than that, it lends to the situation an opportunity that was previously absent.

It would be more precise to say that the moving line tells you where you might possibly go. This added conditional bonus — and every person who draws hexagrams knows how exciting it is to obtain at least one moving line in the operation — tells one that one is tending toward such and such a future if conditions remain the way they are.

It is left up to the person for whom the hexagram is done to fulfill or deny the prophecy. If the prophecy is a good one, for instance, the *I Ching* is indirectly asking the person to fulfill it. If the prophecy is somewhat negative, the person is being indirectly asked to avert it if he or she can. This is one of the greatest challenges to come from the world of the *I Ching* — "Take it or leave it, as you will."

I have witnessed a number of bad prophecies that have been very fortunately nipped in the bud. For example, I once obtained hexagram 47, *OPPRESSION,* with the top line changing. The text said that I would be swamped by "creeping vines" if I did not take a healthier look at what was "oppressing" me. If I failed, the hexagram would mutate into number 6, *CONFLICT.* By forcing myself to encompass this healthier viewpoint, I believe I averted what could have been a very nasty conflict. The next hexagram

I received instead of *CONFLICT* was *DIFFICULTY AT THE BEGINNING*–not nearly so difficult to deal with.

Likewise, I have obtained hexagrams that led to good prophecies. I once obtained hexagram 29, the *ABYSMAL*, with the third line changing. The advice was to be patient. If I followed this advice, I would obtain hexagram 48, *THE WELL.* I did the best I could to follow this advice and eventually found that what I had thought was an abyss was indeed a well of unexpected and fulfilling nourishment. This was connected very closely with the woman I eventually married, so you can see how important it was for me to see deeply into the changes indicated.

The above examples were two of the best I can remember. Others have not always been so clear. If the message of the text led only to *another* good, bad, or "neutral" hexagram, I often found myself a bit stymied.

But this is where the *I Ching* has the greatest potential of encouraging an intuitive drive for wisdom in the user. One must sometimes meditate a great deal to determine whether one *wants* to fulfill the prophecy. One must feel out the surroundings, feel out the opinions of loved ones, and generally just pay exceedingly crucial attention to the overall flow of life that happens to be at one's fingertips at the time.

That the *I Ching* not only allows, but fully encourages, such activities is one of its great virtues. This particular element has led me to respect it more than some of the other synchronistic systems. Astrology is by no means as free with its clients. But for a few notable exceptions in truly great astrologers — and I was privileged to know one such man personally — this synchronistic science tends pretty much to be used to lay down the pattern of one's life in fixed stages or events.

Truly great astrologers are careful to allow a sense of freedom to mix with their ideas. They speak of trends and roadmaps, rather than events and junctions, and they are generally more successful than astrologers who try to do more. The little columns printed in newspapers are a good example of what I mean by the type of shoddiness that is allowed to pass for science. There are approximately 300,000,000 people in the world born under the sign of Pisces. I resent being absorbed into that kind of anonymity when the issue at stake is my destiny. Can you imagine what would happen if all of us fish were to follow the daily columns? Poor world!

Another aspect of the moving, or changing, line arises from its mathematical basis. A changing line is a rarer event than a stable line. As such, it stands for the improbable in life more than a stable line does. It emphasizes the notion of *creative instability* more than anything else that the *I Ching* has to offer. Creative instability is almost a redundancy. All creativity is by nature unstable, since it sets for itself the awesome task of transforming the old into the new or transforming nothingness into some-thingness. Births or any sort are always great un-dertakings. The responsibility involved in any great transformation — such as that which is signified by the changing line — calls for a special and personal commitment to meet its demands.

Special attention ought always to be given to a female moving line. Since this is three times more unusual than the changing male line, its occurrence should always be considered to be of great signifi-cance.

It is your author's opinion that a female change in a usually unimportant place of the hexagram is of more value to the result than a male change found even in the place of rulership. Since this is only a generalization, judgment should always proceed from the hexagram taken as a whole.

The following are several good rules of thumb to entertain in interpreting the relative weights of *two* or more changing lines occurring in a single hexa-gram.

1. Male-female.   Unless the male change occurs in the position of rulership, a female change should nearly always be given priority.

2. Male-male   Between two male changing lines, greater priority should be given to the one occupying rulership. If neither occupies the rulership position, a male line in the first, third, or fifth position is more significant.

3. Female-female   Between two female changing lines, greater priority should be given to the one occupying rulership. Barring this, the second, fourth, and sixth positions have greater weight.

4. In hexagrams of more than two changing lines, only the rulership position has any claim to priority.

Of course, if a hexagram has three or more changing lines, this fact in itself is a matter of crucial importance. Under the philosophy of hexagram families discussed in the last chapter, we can add one further point — the further a hexagram strays from its original family (up to and including the antigram), the more commitments must be undertaken to ensure smooth passage.

A hexagram possessing more than two changing lines is indeed a rare occurrence, and its implications of instability are great. Five and six changing lines at once reveal, in particular, a situation about to undergo changes of the most drastic sort. A person who draws a hexagram of such structure would do well to meditate on his or her situation heavily and expect even the most unpredictable surprises to come about.

In hexagrams with exactly two lines changing, we may consider the possibility of "phantom" hexagrams arising in the transition between the original and the finally mutated hexagrams.

Let us suppose that we have obtained hexagram 12, *STANDSTILL,* with the third and sixth lines changing. The mutated hexagram after both lines change is 31, *INFLUENCE.* But with two lines changing, is it not possible that the advice offered by the two lines could be taken serially? That is, suppose I follow the advice of the third line before I follow that of the sixth–or vice versa. The two "phantom" hexagrams that arise as a result of only one of the two lines' moving would be 45, *GATHER-ING TOGETHER,* or 33, *RETREAT*–obviously two very distinct notions of transition.

Thus a decision must be made based on three possibilities. If the advice of both lines may be taken simultaneously — and in the great majority of cases, this is possible — the full mutation may occur in one stroke. Diagramatically, the above example would be represented as

```
                         6th
    H 12, Standstill ---------→ H 31, Influence
                         3rd
```

But if we take them serially, two more possibilities open up.

H 12 ---$\underline{6th}$--> H 45, Gathering Together ----$\underline{3rd}$--> H 31

or

H 12 -----$3rd$------>H 33, Retreat -----$6th$------> H 31

The intermediary transition hexagrams (45 and 33 in this case) provide pivot points to smooth the rite of passage.

Interestingly enough, the possibilities when more than two lines are changing tend to mushroom out beyond control. With three lines changing, the number of possible routes of mutation is 16. The number of mutations possible in moving from a hexagram to its respective antigram (that is, all six lines changing) is 4,096! It would be very unreasonable to attempt to plan within the scope of these variations.

But the situation of two changing lines offers a unique experimental challenge, and I would hope that interested students will take to it — if not as a matter of conscious planning, then simply as a matter of record. It takes only a moment to note the pivot hexagrams and a simple matter of observation to note whether either of the transitional states happens to arise in one's life while journeying to the fully mutated result.

Now we are ready to discuss a far greater use of creativity with the *Book of Changes.*

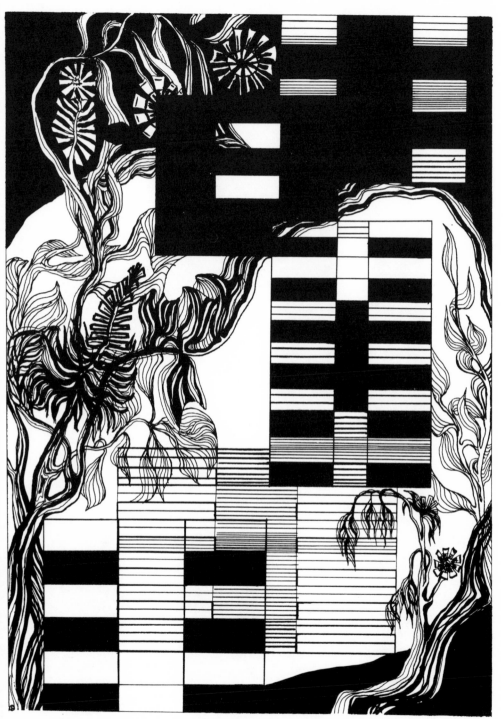

all hexagrams mutate in accord with the time

CHAPTER EIGHT

Creativity and Change

Now that we have discussed some of the ways in which unstable hexagrams mutate into stable hexagrams through the vehicle of the changing line, let us return to the mechanics of the stable hexagram.

To return to the analogy of the chemical elements, we can now say that we have an image of both types of hexagrams that corresponds to the physical world. The stable hexagram exhibits properties of the atom; the unstable, changing hexagram exhibits properties of the ion. The atom is at rest; the ion is tense. The atom is strong and somewhat final; the ion is ephemeral and weak.

But even the hardiest atom will change if the

conditions are right (through fission or fusion). Does anything in the world of the *I Ching* correspond to the breakdown of a stable atom? This is the question we now address.

If I draw hexagram 6, *CONFLICT,* with no lines changing, it obviously doesn't mean that this will always be my hexagram. Eventually I will pass through a few more of life's portals and turn up smiling in the midst of the *JOYOUS* or *PEACE* or *PROGRESS* or some such dream.

So what we must say is that *no hexagram is so stable that it has a terminal effect on the flow of life.* All hexagrams mutate, some more assertively or subtly than others, because life's basic condition of existence is change. And the *I Ching,* as I've said, has been constructed and sustained in the spirit of life.

What I am suggesting is the possibility of consciously working on a hexagram to stimulate its conversion to some other hexagram.

Let us simply say that I want to be in such and such a state — *PUSHING UPWARD,* for instance. Let us furthermore assume that I sit down and in fact obtain hexagram 12, *STANDSTILL. STANDSTILL* is where I am; *PUSHING UPWARD* is where I desire to be. What I have indirectly asked the oracle during the consultation is, "How far am I from *PUSHING UPWARD?* " Diagramatically, this would be represented as

Standstill

```
————————
————————
————————
——  ——
——  ——
——  ——
```

Pushing Upward

```
——  ——
——  ——
——  ——
————————
————————
——  ——
```

The answer shows that I am really quite a distance from where I want to be — five whole changing lines away.

Now, it may be that I have been given changing lines to work with or I haven't. If I have, I use those changing lines to begin my journey to *PUSHING UPWARD*. But suppose I haven't? This is where my theory of creative mutation comes into play. If I have no changing lines, I *create* changing lines. By this, I really mean that I choose to follow the advice of some particular changing line to begin the psychic movement toward *PUSHING UPWARD*.

To do this in legitimate earnest, I must first of all note two things. To begin, I must see if any of the offered changing lines of *STANDSTILL* offer something both meaningful to my present situation and pursuable. Second, I must consult the six hexagrams of *STANDSTILL*'s first family to pick a suitable bridge.

To continue our example in sufficient detail, the

six hexagrams in the first family of *STANDSTILL* are

>   20, *CONTEMPLATION*
>   35, *PROGRESS*
>   45, *GATHERING TOGETHER*
>   25, *INNOCENCE*
>   6, *CONFLICT*
>   33, *RETREAT*

Each of these six hexagrams represents a result of *STANDSTILL* with one of its lines moving. Now, besides consulting the text of changing lines and feeling out the judgments of the resulting hexagrams, I must also take the idea of entropy into account. Hexagrams 20, 35, and 45 are the products of male changes. Hexagrams 25, 6, and 33 are those of female changes. *All other things being equal,* one of the male changes should be adopted, since the transformation will require only one-third as much energy. This is assuming a love of leisure, of course. Your author's inclinations are obviously prejudicing the matter! Workhorses are entitled to any line they wish. In many cases, work or not, a female change may seduce the proper intent of the requirements of the time and ask us to follow her. It is often the case as well (and I frankly don't understand the peculiarity) that female changes are more interesting than male. At any rate, these are some of the issues involved in the change.

128

In this hypothetical case, I have chosen 35, *PROGRESS*, which can be logically incorporated into the goal of *PUSHING UPWARD*. It can be effectively arrived at by following the advice of *STANDSTILL*'s fifth line, and it involves the relatively simpler route of the male change.

The hexagram pursued after *PROGRESS* can be approached in the same manner. The six possibilities this time are

16, *ENTHUSIASM*

12, *STANDSTILL*

23, *SPLITTING APART*

56, *THE WANDERER*

64, *BEFORE COMPLETION*

21, *BITING THROUGH*

This time my inclination is toward *ENTHUSIASM*. However, we must be constantly alert for natural relationships and parallels between the environment and these freely chosen mutations.

Suppose an opportunity arises to do some traveling alone. To take full advantage of this obviously synchronistic parallel, I should side with hexagram 56, *THE WANDERER*, instead. Even though *THE WANDERER* comes about through a female change (*ENTHUSIASM*, through a male change) and is perhaps not as "attractive" as *ENTHUSIASM*, *THE WANDERER* is in tune with the demands of the time. It asks that I make a synchronistic bow by taking to the road. The female lines are going to have to change eventually anyway, as far as that small matter is concerned.

Without going into the details of further mutations, let me just present the hypothetical sequence that I eventually arrived at.

```
                         5th
H 12, Standstill ---------→ H 35, Progress

                         3rd
H 35, Progress ---------→ H 56, The Wanderer

                           2nd
H 56, The Wanderer ---------→ H 50, The Cauldron

                       4th
H 50, The Cauldron ------→ H 18, Work on What
                                  Has Been Spoiled

H 18, Work on What       6th
        Has Been Spoiled ------→ H 46, Pushing Upward
```

Since no line may be changed twice during these transformations, the field of possibilities continues to diminish as the goal hexagram is approached. In the above case, *THE CAULDRON* offered only *DURATION* besides *WORK ON WHAT HAS BEEN SPOILED* as pivots to *PUSHING UPWARD.*

I recognize some of the objections which might be raised against this theory of creative mutation, so let me attempt to answer them as best I can.

To begin with, how does one know that a changing line can be created where one does not, by fate,

130

exist? The answer lies in a mixture of good judgment and strong faith — good judgment in picking a line that could apply to one's life and strong faith in the *I Ching*'s organic solidity.

The second problem is more difficult. How does one know when each transition is reached? This cannot be effectively answered on an objective plane. It ought to be recognized that the above example was rather extreme. The average number of required mutations would probably hardly ever involve more than two transition hexagrams, and this wouldn't be nearly so hard to handle as the example I used. The question of time, however, would have to be handled subjectively in any event.

In *Ta Chuan,* Confucius gives us a sequence that I respect a great deal. I have chosen to discuss this sequence in bringing my treatise to a close. It is called the *character sequence.*

The character sequence is fundamentally irrational. By that, I mean only that I have not found any pattern within it that indicates that it is rooted in some mathematical or structural framework. Therefore, it belongs to the realm of free relations. Its only viability arises on the ground that it sprang from the intuitive workings of the great mind of Confucius.

To quote *Ta Chuan* directly, from the Wilhelm-Baynes translation,

Thus the hexagram of *TREADING* shows the basis of character. *MODESTY* shows the handle of character; *RETURN,* the stem of character. *DURATION* brings about firmness of character; *DECREASE,* cultivation of character; *INCREASE,* fullness of character; *OPPRESSION,* the test of character; *THE WELL,* the field of character; *THE GENTLE,* the exercise of character.

These nine hexagrams are meant to represent guideposts for the self-actualizing human being. They are presented in transcending stages of coming to terms with reality and therefore can be used as a sort of measuring stick of the psyche.

As a matter of interest, I once asked the *I Ching* what it thought of Jesus. I received hexagram 57, *THE GENTLE.* Not until I read this section of *Ta Chuan* did I realize that this hexagram was regarded as the ultimate fulfillment of character.

Besides noting these nine hexagrams when they happen to occur in divination, I would also advise using them in creative mutation whenever possible. What better bridge to use than a bridge of good character?

It is ironic that I have now come down to the *I Ching* as a book of wisdom, rather than a book of oracles. Only one last step can be added to the above discussion. If the goal hexagram can be posited, and all the lines of the original hexagram be chosen freely, why can't the original hexagram be posited too?

The truth is, it can! And this is the *Book of Changes* finally defrocked of any mystical powers beyond its natural wisdom. Do you wish to know what the ancients felt about joy? Read hexagram 58. Do you feel yourself to be in a situation that involves quite a number of initial birth pains? See if *DIFFICULTY AT THE BEGINNING* has something to say to you.

In the last analysis, students will be most required to search their faith in the cohesiveness of the *Book of Changes* as it stands, prior to any oracular possibilities. If they do not satisfy themselves on this basic level, they might as well lay the *I Ching* aside for a while. But if they at least remain open to this faith, experience will surely solidify it for them. And experience is what the *I Ching* claims to understand more than anything. Life writes its own "book of changes" on each page of our long line of experiences. The *I Ching* casts the light upon the page.

Postscript

In the relatively brief period it took to write this book, I have been amazed to witness the fantastic growth in America of interest in things supernatural. And by that term, I mean *super*natural — matters involving Mother Nature in her most elegant array. (I say *elegant,* I suppose, because I feel that this area of nature study offers the richest rewards.) Where I have not seen an overt interest in these things, I have at least seen a much higher tolerance level for discussion of the supernatural in general. I feel that, for perhaps the first time among civilized and rational humanity, outright skeptics represent a minority opinion.

And why shouldn't they? We've seen too much. We've seen an astronaut return from the moon and open up an institute for psychic research. We've watched famous psychics solve incredibly mysterious murder cases. We've seen (as well as photographed) people doing everything from levitating small objects to successfully materializing and dematerializing them. We've noted the growth of acupuncture practice (which originally evolved from the *I Ching*, I understand) against a highly skeptical medical profession too proud to admit that it might have overlooked a whole *system* in the human body. We've seen Kirlian photographs suggest that the ancient occult notion of the aura might have a foundation in modern physics.

To all this, let us add the personal accounts of astral projection, kundalini yoga, spiritualism, UFO contacts, reincarnation, orgone therapy, prophecy, and a host of other unusual but fairly widespread claims. Who but the most narrow-minded would not feel privileged to live in an era of discovery barraged by so many new and marvelous alternatives?

The *I Ching*'s role in this renaissance is unique. Sandwiched between the purely abstract on the one hand and the rawly physical on the other, it plays at being a cross between an industrious gatekeeper and a watchful wizard. Its mere existence as a highly specialized order of synchronistic patterns is enough to let it stand proudly in the emerging world view.

I am hoping that the *I Ching* will play a more direct role, however. Perhaps with the use of the *I*

Ching computer, ways may be found to use the *Book of Changes* in the psychic-research laboratory as a "consultant."

By and large, though, its greater use will surely continue to be what it has always been — as a personal significator. And why shouldn't it? The *I Ching*'s intense subjectivity limits its use in the strictly scientific sphere; yet what more could one ask for, when reaching with all one's heart toward a great vision?

The *I Ching* is one good source of inspired knowledge. There may even be times when it appears as *the* source of inspired knowledge. However far it extends, it extends with great benefit. I know one secret about it already. Its headwaters are fed with an ingredient so fresh and original that the most remote tributaries of the Changes are purified with it. This magic ingredient is irreplaceable and indestructible. I've even heard it go by your name.

SUPPLEMENTARY MATERIAL

Appendix A

Divination Methods

I. The Yarrow-stalk Method

    1. Fifty stalks, sticks, or any conveniently movable items are utilized.

    2. One stalk is put aside and not used again.

    3. The forty-nine remaining stalks are divided into two random heaps.

    4. A stalk is taken from the right heap and placed between the ring finger and the little finger of the left hand.

    5. The left heap is counted through, four stalks at a time, until four or fewer stalks remain. This remainder is placed between

the middle finger and the ring finger of the left hand.

6. The right heap is now counted through in the same manner until four or fewer stalks remain.

7. The remainders are all gathered together, counted, and laid aside as pile *A*. (The quantity should be five or nine.)

8. The first two heaps are gathered together and randomly separated again.

9. Steps 4 through 7 above are repeated twice more (the remainders from each of these totaling four or eight).

10. The three remainder piles (*A, B, C*) are then examined to ascertain the line. The following table shows all the possibilities.

9, 8, 8	(female changing)	— — •
5, 4, 4	(male changing)	—— •
9, 8, 4	(male)	——
9, 4, 8	(male)	——
5, 8, 8	(male)	——
9, 4, 4	(female)	— —
5, 4, 8	(female)	— —
5, 8, 4	(female)	— —

11. Steps 3 through 10 are then repeated five more times to obtain the full hexagram.

II. The Coin Method

1. Three coins are utilized.

2. It is determined in advance whether the heads will be counted as *2* and the tails as *3*, or vice versa.

3. The three coins are thrown into the air and allowed to fall randomly upon a flat surface.

4. The following permutations determine the line received.

5. Step 3 is repeated five more times to obtain the hexagram.

2, 2, 2	———— •
2, 2, 3	— —
2, 3, 2	— —
2, 3, 3	————
3, 2, 2	— —
3, 2, 3	————
3, 3, 2	————
3, 3, 3	— — •

III. The Six-wands Method

1. Six wooden slats are used. Yin lines are painted on one side, yang lines on the other.

2. The six slats are thrown randomly on the ground in front of one.

3. The hexagram is recorded as it appears to the eye (the closest slat being the bottom line, etc.).

4. With this method, no changing lines can be obtained.

APPENDIX B

Mathematical
Calculations

I. The probabilities of Individual Lines

Five stalks are three times more likely to be obtained on the first count than nine stalks. This gives rise to the following permutations:

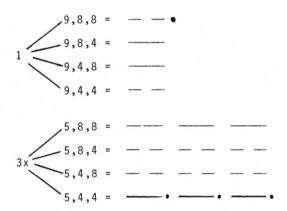

These permutations then result in the following probabilities for individual lines:

— — •   1/16

——— •   3/16

———   5/16

— —   7/16

II. Determining the Probabilities of Stable Hexagrams

```
Stable yin line = 7/16
Stable yang line = 5/16
```

Conversion equation: $Hp = N(7/16^f \times 5/16^m)$

The Creative (Group I) $= 1 \times (5/16)^6$

The Receptive (Group II) $= 1 \times (7/16)^6$

Any hexagram of 1 yin/5 yang (Group III) =
$$6 \times (7/16)(5/16)^5$$

Any hexagram of 2 yin/4 yang (Group IV) =
$$15 \times (7/16)^2 \times (5/16)^4$$

Any hexagram of 5 yin/1 yang (Group V) =
$$6 \times (7/16)^5 \times (5/16)$$

Any hexagram of 3 yin/3 yang (Group VI) =
$$20 \times (7/16)^3 \times (5/16)^3$$

Any hexagram of 4 yin/2 yang (Group VII) =
$$15 \times (7/16)^4 \times (5/16)^2$$

APPENDIX C

Schematic Design for the DNR-16

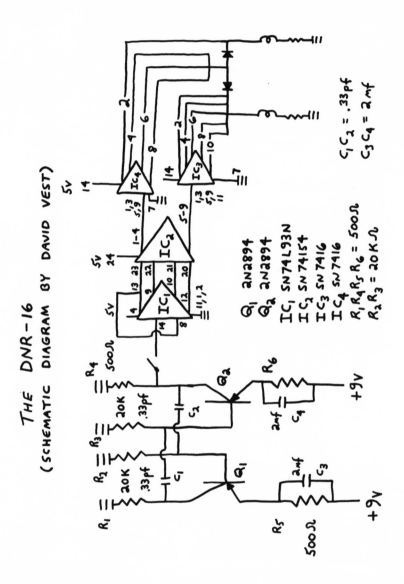

THE DNR-16
(SCHEMATIC DIAGRAM BY DAVID VEST)

$C_1 C_2 = .33\mu f$
$C_3 C_4 = 2\mu f$

Q_1 2N2894
Q_2 2N2894

IC_1 SN74L93N
IC_2 SN74154
IC_3 SN7416
IC_4 SN7416

$R_1, R_4, R_5, R_6 = 500\Omega$
$R_2, R_3 = 20K\Omega$

Bibliography

I Ching: A New Interpretation for Modern Times, by Sam Reifler, Bantam, 1974.

I Ching: Book of Changes, Ed. by Ch'u Chai & Winberg Chai, Tr. by James Legge, University Books, 1964.

I Ching: The Book of Changes, Tr. by John Blofeld, E.P. Dutton, 1968.

The I Ching or Book of Changes, Tr. by C.F. Baynes & R. Wilhelm, Princeton University Press, 1967.

Change: Eight Lectures on the I Ching, by Hellmut Wilhelm, Tr. by C.F. Baynes, Princeton University Press, 1972.

The New Dictionary of Thoughts, Ed. by Ralph Emerson Brown, Standard Book Co., 1960.

Principles of Change: Understanding the I Ching, by Jung Young Lee, University Books, 1971.

Synchronicity: An Acausal Connecting Principle, by Carl G. Jung, Princeton University Press, 1960.

Index

Alpha Centauri, 36
Antigrams, 99–102
Astrology, 46, 62, 64, 116

Beethoven, 36
Bergson, Henri 24
Big Bang theory, 64
Blofeld, John 100
Bone oracle, 76

Character sequence, 131–132
Chuang-tsu, 48
Coin method, 82, 143
Collective Unconscious, 39
Confucius, 23, 47–49, 77, 131

Duke of Chou, 76

Einstein, 24, 36, 65
Elan Vitale, 24
Electric media, 27
Emerson, 29
Entropy, 66, 81–82, 95, 128
ESP, 68–69
Evolution, 57–58, 66–67
Evolutionary energy, 24
Existentialism, 35, 40

First families, 105–106

Gardner, Martin, 80
General Theory of Relativity, 65

Heisenberg, 65
Hexagrams,
  compared to atoms, 89, 125
  individually remarked upon,
      THE CREATIVE, 90–95, 99–101
      THE RECEPTIVE, 90–95, 99–101
      DIFFICULTY AT THE BEGINNING, 100,
         115, 133
      YOUTHFUL FOLLY, 102
      CONFLICT, 114–115, 126
      THE ARMY, 101, 105
      TREADING, 132
      PEACE, 126
      STANDSTILL, 93, 119–120, 126–130
      FELLOWSHIP WITH MEN, 54, 101, 105
      POSSESSION IN GREAT MEASURE, 94
      MODESTY, 132
      ENTHUSIASM, 100, 129
      WORK ON WHAT HAS BEEN SPOILED,
         130
      APPROACH, 101
      CONTEMPLATION, 128
      BITING THROUGH, 55, 129
      SPLITTING APART, 129
      RETURN, 132
      INNOCENCE, 128

THE ABYSMAL, 115
INFLUENCE, 119–120
DURATION, 130, 132
RETREAT, 101, 120, 128
PROGRESS, 126
THE FAMILY, 102
DELIVERANCE, 55–56, 102
DECREASE, 132
INCREASE, 132
GATHERING TOGETHER, 119–120
PUSHING UPWARD, 126–130
OPPRESSION, 114, 132
THE WELL, 115, 132
REVOLUTION, 102
THE CAULDRON, 130
THE WANDERER, 129
THE GENTLE, 132
THE JOYOUS, 55, 126
AFTER COMPLETION, 101
BEFORE COMPLETION, 101, 129
    meditations upon, 133
    phantom hexagrams, 119–120
    sequences of, 106–108, 131
Hippocrates, 61

I Ching,
    as a book of wisdom, 49, 132–133
    creative uses of, 113–133
    general history of, 45–53
    intelligence behind, 56–58
    mathematics of, 77–95, 146–147
    personal history with, 54–58

Jeans, Sir James, 65
Jesus, 132
Jung, Carl, 39, 53, 61–64

King Wen, 76
Krishna, Gopi, 24

Lao Nai-hsuan, 47
Lao-tse, 23–24, 32, 35
Lee, Jung Young, 89
Legge, James, 53
Leibniz, 52–53

Moving lines, 100–107, 113–121

Paragrams, 102–103
Periodic table, 91–96, 105
Pisces, 116
Probability theory, 56, 65

Quantum mechanics, 51, 65

Radioactive decay, 64–65

Sartre, Jean-Paul, 35
Scorpius, 62
Second Law of Thermodynamics, 81–82
Self-actualizing man, 132
Shao Yung, 49–52, 106
Shepard, Leslie, 31, 56
Sixteen-System, 81–85

Six wands method, 76, 144
Skinner, B.F., 34
Space-time continuum, 64
Suzuki, D.T., 24
Synchronicity Principle, 57, 61–69

Ta Chuan (The Great Treatise), 49, 77, 131–132

Uncertainty Principle, 65
Unified Field Theory, 24, 65

Wang Pi, 49
Wilhelm, Hellmut, 52–53, 80–81
Wilhelm, Richard, 46–47, 53–54, 77, 79, 100

Yarrow stalk method, 45–48, 76–84, 141–142